CRACKING THE
SALES CODE

The Secret Formula to Unlock Your Sales
Potential in Business Sales

AUSTIN MACAULEY PUBLISHERS™
LONDON • CAMBRIDGE • NEW YORK • SHARJAH

Copyright © Hassan Al Ali 2022

The right of **Hassan Al Ali** to be identified as author of this work has been asserted by the author in accordance with Federal Law No. (7) of UAE, Year 2002, Concerning Copyrights and Neighboring Rights.

All rights reserved. No part of this publication may be reproduced, stored in a retrieval system, or transmitted in any form or by any means, electronic, mechanical, photocopying, recording, or otherwise, without the prior permission of the publishers.

Any person who commits any unauthorized act in relation to this publication may be liable to legal prosecution and civil claims for damages.

The age category suitable for the books' contents has been classified and defined in accordance to the Age Classification System issued by the National Media Council.

ISBN – 9789948817888 - (Paperback)
ISBN – 9789948817895 -   (E-Book)

Application Number: MC-10-01-6227093
Age Classification: E

Printer Name: Al Nisr Publishing LLC
Printer Address: Dubai, United Arab Emirates

First Published 2022
AUSTIN MACAULEY PUBLISHERS FZE
Sharjah Publishing City
P.O Box [519201]
Sharjah, UAE
www.austinmacauley.ae
+971 655 95 202

Dedication:

This book is dedicated to all the salespeople who strive to excel, day in and day out. It does not matter whether they are affected by a recession or working through the COVID-19 pandemic that rocked the world. They are the heroes of any organization—the ones who face tough buyers and work on a deal that takes months, if not years, to close, and are still committed to hanging in there. Unlike any other profession, salespeople put their salary on the line—and never rest until they deliver their target. Hats off to you. Keep going.

ACKNOWLEDGMENT

To my parents. Thank you for the support throughout these years and for remembering me in your prayers. None of this would have been possible without you. God bless you.

To my little family (UmKhalid, Khalid, Reem, and Majed). Thank you for believing in me and being there for me, no matter what. I must say, putting up with me is a little hard sometimes. I am blessed to have you all in my life.

To my brothers and sisters. It has been an exciting journey together. Thank you for your support.

To my friends. Thank you for challenging my ideas to get the best out of me. You guys rock.

To the Preferred Business Sales team. Thank you for your dedication and the unconditional support to get the team to the top.

To the Channel Partner team. It has been great exposure to work with a large sales team and drive results together. It was fun working with all of you.

And finally, to the Etisalat leadership team. Thank you for allowing me to grow personally and professionally.

CONTENTS

Acknowledgment	v
Foreword	ix
My Sales Journey	xiii
Part I Sales Is Science	xix
Chapter 1 The MST Framework	21
Chapter 2 From Mediocrity to Top Performance	25
Chapter 3 Sales Framework	37
Chapter 4 Why Do Salespeople Struggle?	43
Part II Mindset	**31**
Chapter 5 Success Begins with Mindset	53
Chapter 6 Mindset #1 – Discipline	59
Chapter 7 Mindset #2 – Proactivity	81
Chapter 8 Mindset #3 – Positivity	91
Chapter 9 Mindset #4 – Persistence	99
Chapter 10 Mindset #5 – Relationships	107
Chapter 11 Mindset #6 – Growth	117
Chapter 12 Mindset Reflection	123

Part III Skillset   **127**

    Chapter 13 Sales Combat Zone   129

    Chapter 14 The Sales Story   133

    Chapter 15 Sales Story Structure   137

    Chapter 16 Sales Pipeline Management   177

    Chapter 17 Pipeline Buildup   179

    Chapter 18 Pipeline Balance   189

    Chapter 19 Pipeline Velocity   203

    Chapter 20 Pipeline Product Mix   211

    Chapter 21 Sales Pipeline Mistakes to Avoid   215

Part IV Toolset   **219**

    Chapter 22 Product Share of Wallet   221

    Chapter 23 Sales Business Plan   231

Conclusion   **239**

Appendix   **243**

References   **256**

FOREWORD

I assume you are familiar with what happens on battlefields. The battalion with the best equipment, preparation, and strategy, is likely to win the battle. Leaders don't send troops out to a combat zone without the right weapons and training to take the enemy down. Sales is no different: the more prepared the salespeople, the higher the chances of winning new businesses.

I have been in the company of salespeople for the past twenty years, and I currently fill the role of senior vice president of SMB (small and medium business) at Etisalat-UAE. I have come across numerous star players, and, at the same time, I have met many salespeople who struggle to hit their monthly targets. Such disparity is surprising because the resources available to all salespeople are the same. So why do we see some salespeople delivering reliably and others failing miserably?

Sales can be easy, and I personally believe that with the right sales formula, everyone in sales should reach the summit of success they dream of. However, success doesn't come walking to you; you have to step out of your comfort zone to reach out to it. That is exactly why you should read this book—everything that you need to know about success in business sales is covered in a comprehensive way.

Hassan has been on my team for the past fifteen years. When he took over the sales helm in 2015, I knew that it would not be an easy task, as we were heading toward uncharted territory. Despite all the challenges, he successfully revolutionized the way sales was managed, and he was able to bring about a big turnaround across all channel partners in a way no one thought was possible. The book in your hand shares how the journey started and the secret formula behind his exponential success.

This book is a simple guide for learning how to be a successful sales professional. It provides an effective formula that clears out all the confusion around success in sales. I strongly believe that no one in sales should struggle after reading this book, and no one should have an excuse not to succeed, regardless of which industry they operate in. The formula is straightforward and easy to implement, and I wish this information had been available to all salespeople long ago.

The book revolves around three broad categories: mindset, skillset, and toolset. With the endless challenges that you face in sales, your mindset is the only savior, and it is a key component in propelling you forward. However, mindset alone is not enough to guarantee success. Mindset has to be paired with the right skillset. Sharpening your skillset and equipping yourself with the right weapons is what this book is all about. Being prepared for small skirmishes in sales is essential to win the final battle in the marketplace. In addition to a growth-oriented mindset and skillset, toolset is also a basic necessity in the sales domain. It enables salespeople to target the *right* customers at the *right* time, selling the *right* product. Linking these three pieces together paves the way toward a successful career in sales.

Follow the sales success formula in this book, and you will surely be triumphant. Master the formula to unlock a host of new possibilities and opportunities. There is no better time to begin your sales journey. Go out there and start winning BIG.

Esam Mahmoud

Senior Vice President, SMB

Etisalat-UAE

MY SALES JOURNEY

I love sales, and I have been working with frontline salespeople for the past fifteen years. I have seen the good, the bad, and the ugly. I have come across many relationship managers (RMs) who excel consistently and show resilient performance throughout the year. I have also dealt with mediocre ones who ride performance rollercoasters throughout the year. Their contribution to the team is doubtful; one month is up, while several months are down. I am sure you have seen these people around, and trust me, you don't want to be one of them.

The performance variation in sales is outrageous, partly because the resources available to all sales reps are the same. The culture, the management, the tools, and the environment are exactly the same. Yet we see a clear difference in performance between the top achievers and the average players. For a long time, I have pondered the reason for the performance gap between the two groups of salespeople. I was always curious to know what top performers do that others don't and whether their method could be replicated and taught to the rest of the team to be as productive and efficient as the top achievers.

As vice president of SMB sales in Etisalat-UAE, I have the privilege of working with a supercharged sales team of sixty salespeople who are crushing their monthly quota, despite all the challenges they face on a daily basis. I have observed the team in action, and I can say with 100 percent certainty that I have the answers to what it takes to become a successful sales professional. I will be sharing my experience as a salesperson as well as the secret sauce of the ultra-high performers and their unique way of over-achieving their goals. This book will explore practical ideas that can be implemented on the ground right away, with no theories involved. It is your definitive guide and companion for a journey to success.

Success doesn't need to be out of reach, even if you are brand new in sales. You just need to set yourself up for success by getting three fundamental things right:

1) Mindset

2) Skillset

3) Toolset

This book will take you on an exciting adventure to explore the secrets of the MST (Mindset, Skillset, Toolset) framework, enabling you to become an ultra-high performer as you hit your quota every month—while having fun and enjoying a successful career in sales.

This book is divided into four parts. The first part explores the science behind sales. The book's later parts dive deep into the MST framework, stemming from the first element of the MST model, which is the *mindset*. Extraordinary results are possible if this piece of the framework is nurtured. A growth-focused sales mindset separates the ultra-high performers from the average ones. A robust sales mindset is your only armor for all the challenges you will face throughout the sales journey. Embrace a healthy sales mindset and see yourself stand out from the crowd!

Chapters 5 to 12 provide the blueprint for a successful sales career. They focus on the core elements of the sales mindset: discipline, proactivity, positivity, persistence, relationship, and growth.

The second element of the MST framework is the *skillset*. Possessing the right skillset accelerates your success in sales. I have yet to see a successful salesperson who doesn't have the right skillset. Sharpening your skills is key—dare to neglect your sales skills, and mediocrity will tarnish your career.

Chapters 13 to 15 will help you master the essentials of creating a compelling *sales story*. They will show you how to get equipped with the most effective weapon in sales: a systematic approach to building your own sales story from the ground up—for any product or solution you sell. It is so simple that anyone can craft their own sales story to take to market with confidence that it will work.

The second aspect of the sales skillset is mastering the *sales pipeline*. Chapters 16 to 21 will empower you to manage the pipeline, from prospecting to lead closure. Top performers pay attention to four key elements of sales pipeline management: size, balance, velocity, and product mix. Observing these metrics will reveal your strengths and limitations. It will involve identifying the symptoms and prescribing your own remedy to fix any areas of concern.

The last part of the MST framework is the sales *toolset*. The toolset complements the mindset and the skillset. The toolset is either provided to you, or you develop it on your own. We will also discover the benefits of maintaining a comprehensive *product share of wallet* and how it can guide your prospecting efforts. It is a powerful asset that situates you in front of the right customer, at the right time, selling the right product.

The MST framework will, without a doubt, provide a resilient foundation for your sales career if the entire framework is developed as a whole.

The right sales mindset alone cannot guarantee success in sales. The aspect of mindset must be complemented by the right skillset and toolset. On the other hand, exercising the sales skillset without the sales mindset is a recipe for mediocre performance. Your success is only possible if you develop all three aspects at the same time.

You didn't think success would come only by knowing the framework, did you? Of course not. There is another input to the equation—YOU. Success requires discipline and commitment, and the MST formula has to be practiced day in and day out. Failing to implement it is as problematic as never learning it in the first place.

There is no magic formula or silver bullet that will turn your sales career around. Investing in *yourself* is an integral part of success. As we will explore in this book, a high degree of commitment is required on your part. It will not be easy, and it will require a massive investment of time. It is well known that success in sales is not a right—it has to be earned!

I enjoy working with frontline salespeople, especially when it comes to digital sales. Within this book, I will be discussing sales in general, with a laser focus on digital sales in the SMB domain. The MST framework is equally relevant in every other domain. In the end, sales is sales, regardless of the industry you operate in. However, this book will benefit you the most if you manage a set of accounts in a business-to-business setting. To set the right expectations for this book, the relationship with the customer should already be established, since this book does not discuss how to connect with or hunt for new customers.

I have an ambitious goal: transforming the way you approach sales. Once you perfect it, you will have an entire world of opportunities before you. Wield your sales weapon with stark determination and slay the challenges that come your way.

I would like to end this introduction with this bold statement: It does not matter which industry or background you come from. After finishing this book and working on your mindset, skillset, and toolset, you will become a sales expert who can take on any challenge—guaranteed!

Let's dive in and explore how the MST (Mindset, Skillset, and Toolset) framework plants us at the forefront, miles ahead of the rest of the pack.

CRACKING THE SALES CODE

THE SECRET FORMULA TO UNLOCK YOUR SALES POTENTIAL IN BUSINESS SALES

Part I
SALES IS SCIENCE

Chapter 1
THE MST FRAMEWORK

I am not going to paint a rosy picture and tell you that sales is easy. We all know that sales is hard, partly because selling involves other people. It is always you and someone else whom you have to deal with, convince, and covert into a customer. While you can be keenly aware of your own state of mind, it is hard to understand the other party because you are only indirectly dealing with their emotions. That is exactly what makes sales so difficult. However, having the right mindset can put you at a significant advantage.

Consistent and resilient performance in sales was a mystery to many salespeople, including me, but not anymore. In the quest to figure out what it takes to be a successful salesperson, I came across an interesting blog by Steve Jones. The article was about enhancing training methodologies to achieve peak performance by combining mindset, skillset, and toolkit. It immediately occurred to me that addressing these three elements comprehensively in what we do in sales will undoubtedly produce great results. Most relationship managers are either struggling with mindset or skillset or don't have access to the right toolset to achieve their goals. That is exactly why we see a big gap in performance between the top producers and the average ones.

Ultra-high performers know the framework and live by it, and I want you to be among them. Your name should come among those who consistently crush their quota, do not shy away from their true potential, and go beyond after learning the secret sauce that top producers often keep under wraps—the MST framework.

More often than not, we don't take the time to perform a 360-degree evaluation of ourselves. But I am assuming that every salesperson would like to work on their flaws and embrace their strengths. The framework is a good place to start. It indicates which parts of the model we need to fix and develop and which parts we should continue to enhance.

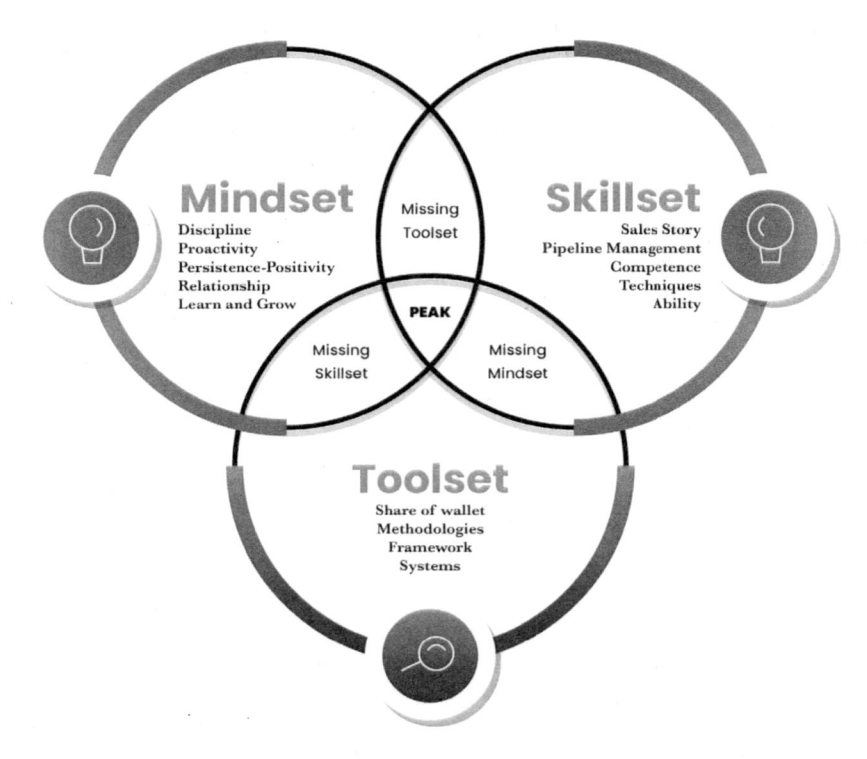

Mindset
Discipline
Proactivity
Persistence-Positivity
Relationship
Learn and Grow

Skillset
Sales Story
Pipeline Management
Competence
Techniques
Ability

Toolset
Share of wallet
Methodologies
Framework
Systems

Missing Toolset
Missing Skillset
Missing Mindset
PEAK

The MST Formula

NOT A ONE-TIME APPROACH

The execution of the framework isn't a one-time approach. Continuous application of the MST framework is vital to achieving great results. Relationship managers (RMs) and the sales management team must ensure that their mindset, skillset, and toolset are in a healthy balance throughout their sales career to take their performance to the next level.

There should be constant coaching between the line manager and the RM. It is a never-ending endeavor, and if you think it's OK to get all the elements right for a moment in time and then forget about them, it is time to rethink your approach.

You may wonder when you will be ready to venture out in the market in terms of your mindset, skillset, and toolset. Let me break it to you: There won't be a point where you can say, "I am 100 percent ready to go to market, and I should stop working on my mindset, skillset, and toolset." As long as you are in sales, continuous learning is key for a successful career.

THE WHOLE IS GREATER THAN THE SUM OF ITS PARTS

Aristotle said, "The whole is greater than the sum of its parts."

A sales mindset complements the skillset and toolset and vice versa. Paying more attention to your skillset without working on your mindset is a recipe for mediocre performance. The same is true for the other two elements of the framework. Paying more attention to one element while disregarding the others won't bring about the results you dream of.

Addressing only the parts that resonate with you may not be the best approach because the framework's elements must go hand in hand—only then will exceptional results be achieved. Average salespeople unintentionally turn a blind eye to how important it is to stitch these three pieces together to create a remarkable performance. They put in the effort to attend one or two training sessions, thinking that they will help. In the short run, the benefits may be evident, but when we are only looking at one piece of the puzzle sporadically, the information learned during those sessions is quickly tossed out the window.

Many companies create a lucrative incentive plan, thinking it will do the job, but they forget about the significance of developing the mindset and skillset of the team. On the other hand, some companies provide a comprehensive toolset and product information yet never pay attention to the other two elements of the equation.

You get the idea. As a sales professional, you should be looking at the MST framework as a whole to reach your true potential, achieve peak performance, and become an elite sales player. As a relationship manager, you hold the responsibility for your success. If the company you work for doesn't provide the support necessary to succeed, you should implement it at your own level. Nothing can stop you from doing it yourself. However, the company culture *does* matter, and great success is possible for a company that rises up and embraces this framework from a holistic perspective.

Chapter 2

FROM MEDIOCRITY TO TOP PERFORMANCE

I like to work closely with salespeople. Meeting with relationship managers every week has been part of my routine for many years, and I plan to continue to meet the team as long as I am in the role of leading frontline salespeople. I prefer to spend time with top achievers and ensure that they reach their true potential. I also like to commit time to average salespeople to figure out their challenges and help turn their performance around.

Meet Ahmed, who works for one of the channel partners. He has been an average performer for the past few months. Ahmed was enthusiastic about sales; however, he was unsure of what to expect the following month, quarter, or year. He was desperate for results and would do anything to hit his target, even if he had to sit in the customer's office for an entire day just to get a signature on the application form. That is not something I like to see.

Ahmed has the passion and motivation to succeed in sales and contribute to his team's success, but unfortunately, he doesn't know how to make it happen. Not knowing how sales works leads to desperation, and salespeople wing it, hoping to stumble upon any deal that comes their way.

Sales is science. If you put the right formula together, I don't see a valid reason why you should struggle in sales. The framework that this book talks about is so replicable and so natural that it helps salespeople master their craft conveniently, provided they have the willingness and motivation to develop and learn.

To turn Ahmed's performance around, I decided to coach him for a week to determine what needed improvement. It is worth mentioning that a week of coaching sessions won't be enough to set the right expectations. Coaching is not a one-time approach. It has to be a constant endeavor. After a week of coaching Ahmed, I handed the task to his line manager to reinforce what Ahmed had learned. Here is how it went.

DAY ONE OF COACHING

Starting the day early in the morning, the first thing I noticed was that Ahmed didn't have anything on his calendar. Absolutely nothing. He left his days open to whatever might suddenly require his time and attention. Sales is crazy with everything that is thrown at you, from customer issues and preparing proposals, to dropping someone off at a nearby location and even sometimes fixing the printer. Salespeople are pulled in different directions and given tasks that have *nothing* to do with sales and are far from having any connection to productive sales-related activities.

Planning at least seven days ahead is something that everyone should follow, simply because if an activity is not booked on your calendar, it won't happen. If you have no clarity on the sales activities that you will work on every hour for the next seven days, don't expect to be a productive salesperson.

Ahmed wasn't lazy. He was just occupied with everything except sales. Ahmed forgot the main goal of sales: generating new business. Keep in mind, anything that does not contribute to your monthly target doesn't have a bearing on your performance, and you have the right to say no—the *duty* to say no. Protect your time and ensure, with 100 percent certainty, that what you do is directly linked to revenue-generating activities—not operations or finance-related tasks. Leave these unrelated sales activities to the relevant people in the organization. They will do a better job since they have a greater understanding of their domain.

Managing Ahmed's calendar was the first step toward helping him become a productive salesperson. We agreed that every Monday, first thing in the morning, he would plan for the following week and fine-tune his schedule, depending on the outcome of each day. We worked out a plan, and here is a list of activities Ahmed agreed to book on his calendar every day for at least seven days:

- Learning and development
- Prospecting for new business over the phone
- Meeting customers virtually
- Meeting customers face-to-face
- Balancing the pipeline
- Looking at customers' issues

- Reading emails
- Other tasks

We also considered time allocation for every activity and agreed that the time allocated for each activity might vary daily, depending on the status of each activity.

Since Ahmed needed a big turnaround across all metrics, we decided on the following:

- One hour of learning and development before the start of work
- Two hours of prospecting over the phone
- One hour of balancing the pipeline
- Four hours of meeting customers virtually and physically
- One hour of clearing emails and addressing customers' issues

After identifying and fixing the calendar gap, the next aspect we focused on was Ahmed's annual goal. Ahmed had a target in mind, but it had been defined by the company. I was more interested in looking at his own quarterly and yearly goals and what plans he had in place to achieve them.

Ahmed didn't have a goal, let alone a plan. He was like many other salespeople, who figure out their goal as they go along. That is not a very sound plan. Think about an airplane captain who makes sure that a plane is flightworthy but is unsure where to fly it. If the captain takes off without knowing where to fly, the airplane will certainly crash, as it will run out of fuel. The same thing is true in sales. If you don't know what your annual goal is, how will you plan your day, week, and month? What kind of activities can you carry out to reach the goal when you don't even know what it is?

Ahmed and I sat down to plan for the current quarter since we were almost done with the year. Based on his current level of performance, we set a reasonable and achievable goal and sketched a blueprint to reach it.

At the end of day one, Ahmed agreed to have a business plan detailing the goal and the activities around achieving the goal.

We agreed on what to include in his business plan, and here is a snippet comprising the important elements. The business plan doesn't have to be too long. It could be two or three pages. We will be discussing how to write up a sales business plan in detail in chapter 23.

- Goal
- Mindset development plan
- Skillset development plan
- Pipeline management plan
- Toolset development plan

DAY TWO OF COACHING

The first day with Ahmed was full of enthusiasm. The attention and level of engagement he exhibited proved that he was keen to take his performance to the next level and contribute to the team's achievement.

The second day of coaching with Ahmed was all about building a growth sales mindset. It is interesting because a sales mindset can either make or break your sales efforts, yet only a few salespeople know their own state of mind. It was no surprise that Ahmed had a strong sales mindset but needed a fresh and new perspective.

Sales is tough. Facing adversity every single day is part of the sales culture. Coping with challenges and setbacks requires mental toughness. However, it doesn't need to be *that* hard. With a little work on building the right mindset, everyone can put the hard times behind them. In most cases, customers will make your sales journey more difficult, but you need to rise above the challenges and overcome them.

Ahmed and I discussed the importance of having a sales-driven mindset that propels salespeople forward, despite adversity, setbacks, and all the challenges present in the quest to unlock our potential. We talked about what comprises a growth sales mindset: things like discipline, proactivity, positivity, persistence, relationships, and growth. All these elements of a sales-driven mindset will be illuminated in detail from chapter 5 to chapter 12.

DAY THREE OF COACHING

The second session with Ahmed seemed akin to a motivational talk, but it was a reflection of reality. We agreed that without a sales-driven mindset, none of the tools or skills you have matter. Having a great skillset is one thing, but utilizing it properly is a different thing. Therefore, it is safe to conclude that the skillset without a sales-driven mindset is valueless.

However, success in sales is not complete if it is not complemented by the right skillset. On my third day with Ahmed, we discussed the skillset necessary to succeed in sales. Here is how the conversation went:

Me: What kind of skillset do you think you should master to reach your potential?

Ahmed: Well, I guess building relationships with customers is important.

Me: Sure, the relationship is extremely important. It will be hard to sell if you don't develop relationships with the clients.

Ahmed: It is also important to have good communication skills.

Me: You are absolutely right. I will let you in on a little secret. If you want to sharpen your skillset, you should work on your sales story. The sales story is the primary skillset to focus on. There are other skillsets that you need in sales, but let's focus on one of the most important skillsets to master in sales.

If you still don't get it, the *sales story* is the sales pitch or sales play. It is a way of delivering your message with a sheer focus on the customer's business in a bid to identify the current state vs. the future state of the customer. Success in sales largely depends on how clear and concise the sales story is. It should be direct and to the point. Most importantly, it should be about the customer. If you get the sales story right, you will find it very easy to have a seamless conversation with the client. You will love engaging with clients because telling stories is more fun than delivering a boring sales pitch.

We spent a full day discussing the main components of the sales story and how to craft it. Fine-tuning the sales story requires many sessions, and it is an ongoing process. We agreed that going to market without a solid sales story is just a total waste of the RM's and the customer's time. Chapters 14 and 15 are all about building your sales story from the ground up through a simple and easy framework.

DAY FOUR OF COACHING

As we got closer to the end of the coaching sessions, I discussed two things with Ahmed: the toolkit and the product share of wallet.

Me: So, Ahmed, tell me: What kind of toolkit do you rely on to create new opportunities?

Ahmed: I have PowerPoint presentations that contain information about the products.

Me: OK, there are many things that you should keep safe in a folder for easy reference, for example, proposals, quotations, sales stories, and product information. However, do you know that many salespeople fail because they repeatedly target the wrong customers until they give up? Getting it right will offer you a competitive advantage over other salespeople.

Ahmed: I am curious. Can you explain this tool in greater detail?

Me: The *product share of wallet* is a necessary tool if you intend to be among the top performers. The product share of wallet is the pre-pipeline stage. The RM should never approach the customer before looking at the share of wallet first. It is an effective way of formulating multiple plans of attack. It makes things easier and simpler. It provides a quick and easy way of creating a strategic list of customers to target for every product in your portfolio. It also helps determine which customer to follow up with consistently and which customer to avoid altogether.

Ahmed: How does it work?

Me: Let me show you how to create it. You will thank me later. (Chapter 22 discusses the product share of wallet in detail.)

THE LAST DAY OF COACHING

They always say, "Save the best for last." The concluding lesson of the coaching session brought up one of the most important tools that a salesperson has at their disposal—pipeline management. We discussed the importance of properly managing and maintaining the pipeline. It is one of the main ingredients for success. Here is how the discussion went:

Me: Today's session is going to be about pipeline management. What do you think about it, and how do you manage it?

Ahmed: Pipeline management is important, and I check my pipeline weekly and sometimes monthly.

Me: Do you think once a week or once a month is sufficient?

Ahmed: I am not sure, but this is what I have seen my colleagues doing.

Me: What do you check in the pipeline?

Ahmed: I usually try to generate new leads and advance them to the next stage.

Me: Great, is that it?

Ahmed: Yes, that's pretty much it.

Me: There are other elements of the pipeline that we should monitor closely. Let me tell you what the best practice is. Here are the four elements of the pipeline that should be proactivity managed:

1) Prospecting: new leads that go into your pipeline.

2) Pipeline balance: all about moving leads from one stage to another.

3) Pipeline velocity: how fast the deals are moving from one stage to the next.

4) Product mix: the health of the pipeline from a diversity perspective. It shows which products you are focusing on and which ones you need to pay attention to.

Managing the four pipeline elements will set you up for success and help you achieve your numbers reliably. The metrics of every pipeline element must be aligned with your monthly target.

Ahmed: That's clear. It makes sense, and I'll start paying attention to these four elements.

Me: A weakness in any of these four elements indicates that something is not going in the right direction. For example, if you are not generating enough leads, it reflects a skillset gap. If the pipeline is full but you are still not closing, it means that your pipeline is not balanced, and all leads are skewed toward the first stage.

The pipeline shows many symptoms of underperformance, and you can immediately make out what the issue is. Diagnosing and prescribing the remedy yourself is necessary to take your performance to the next level. (Chapters 16 and 21 discuss pipeline management in detail.)

Ahmed: Makes sense, thank you.

Me: OK, come here, and let me show you how it works. We will meet next week to check your progress on the elements we have discussed.

The coaching sessions with Ahmed are a point of reflection for many average salespeople, who often commit similar mistakes. Ahmad was either limited by a lack of knowledge or a lack of implementation, a common characteristic of average salespeople. Please remember: Knowing without implementing is as bad as not knowing. Ahmed is now aware of the significance of nurturing a growth mindset, developing the right skillset, and possessing the necessary toolkit in order to be a successful sales professional.

There are now two destinies for Ahmed: give up and go back to his old way of working, or take his sales career seriously and start to work on the MST framework—the same way you can!

Chapter 3

SALES FRAMEWORK

Let's set the right expectations. This book explains sales in general, with a laser focus on digital sales, specifically in the SMB domain. This guide is best suited for a salesperson who manages a set of business accounts in a B2B setting. If you handle customers in the B2C domain, the first and the second parts of the book will prove to be extremely useful, though the third and fourth parts may not provide as many benefits. The realizable advantages depend on the industry in which you operate. However, the book is worth your time, whether your focus is on B2B, B2C or B2G.

To avoid confusion, note that I use the terms *relationship manager*, *RM*, *salesperson, sales rep, sales professional*, and *salespeople* interchangeably throughout the book. I also use *lead, deal,* or *opportunity* the same way.

THE FRAMEWORK

Whether sales is conducted conventionally or digitally, there is a framework to follow. When selling any product, we usually go through five broad steps that dictate an ideal discussion with the client:

- Find the gap
- Bridge the gap
- Capture the product share of wallet
- Advance deals in the pipeline
- Close the deal

Let's explain every stage in turn.

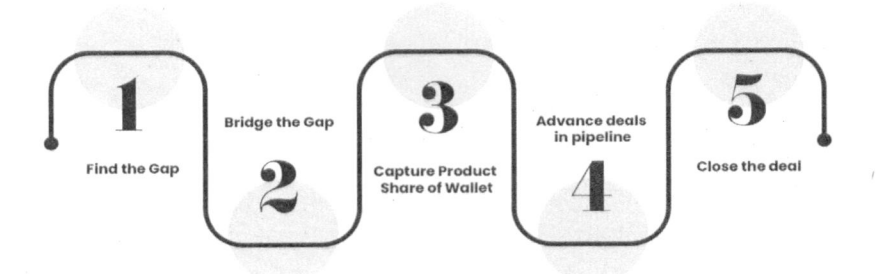

1 Find the Gap
2 Bridge the Gap
3 Capture Product Share of Wallet
4 Advance deals in pipeline
5 Close the deal

The Sales Framework

The framework above sets the stage for an effective sales discussion. It shows where to start and how to end. Skipping stages of the sales process will complicate the discussion with the customer. You can't bridge the gap before identifying it, nor can you jump to closure before managing the stages of the pipeline.

The sequence of the process matters, especially the first two stages, Find the Gap and Bridge the Gap. The latter should not, in any way, precede the former. After all, what can you bridge if you don't know what the gap is?

Have you ever been asked to sell a product? If you have, think about your approach and the focus of your pitch. The mistake that the majority of salespeople make is jumping directly to the closure stage. They usually start by highlighting the product's features and emphasizing its benefits. The problem with this approach is clear: the mediocre salesperson jumps directly to the closure stage and never takes an interest in probing the customer's needs or discovering why the product is needed in the first place. Skipping stages is a primary reason for failure.

The sales process happens in iteration. You could pass the Find the Gap stage but always go back to it for more insight about the customer and their unique situation. The same holds true for the other stages in the sales process until the deal is closed. Let's unpack the stages of the sales framework.

FIND THE GAP

As the name implies, the primary objective of this stage is to find the gap. Assessing the client's initial responses to decide if the client is the right target for the product is crucial. You don't want to be in a situation where you talk about the solution just to find out that the customer is already using a similar product.

Find the Gap is the most important stage in the sales framework. Eighty percent of your time should be spent understanding the customer and their unique situation. It is essential to have a complete awareness of the customer's problems, the impact of these problems on their business, the opportunities they want to capture, and the results they want to achieve.

Discovery is all about the customer's business. God gave us two ears and one mouth. This is exactly how we should behave: listening twice as much as we talk. We should ask open-ended questions to encourage the customer to talk more. The more the customer talks, the more information they will reveal. In my visits alongside relationship managers,

I have been surprised to see how the underperformers cut the customers off and tried to push their point across. Think about it, the customer was trying to pass valuable information that could be capitalized upon, but the salesperson insisted on interrupting them and indirectly said, "I am more important than you. Listen to me and my product." You would probably agree with me that it is a *really* terrible practice. Unfortunately, it is a common practice among the underperformers.

Here's an important lesson to all my fellow salespeople: closing happens in the Find the Gap stage. You can get the customer to agree and say 'yes' to your proposition before even discussing it! It is awesome when customers chase you to find the solution to their problems, as opposed to you pushing your product down their throat.

Skipping the Find the Gap stage in the sales process is detrimental and a huge barrier. The moment that the salesperson jumps to the product's features, consider the deal dead. Remember, the customer's issues and opportunities come first. Your product and solution come second.

In the gap-identification stage, you cannot solve a problem or identify an opportunity without connecting to the right stakeholders. It is essential to level up all the way to CEO, CIO, and other C-level executives. Seek their engagement early in the discussion and watch how your pipeline skyrockets. Average salespeople get glued to one person in the company and never level up to higher management.

BRIDGE THE GAP

Once the gaps have been identified, you are ready to address them, since you now understand the customer's problems and potential opportunities. The outcome of the Find the Gap stage sets the tone for an effective Bridge the Gap stage. A comprehensive and exhaustive discovery will pave the way to a seamless discussion. Your intention is to entice the customer to chase you for a solution to the problems you have identified. Thus, the Bridge the Gap stage should never precede the Find the Gap stage. After all, solutions are meant to address problems. How can you provide a solution for unknown problems?

CAPTURING THE PRODUCT SHARE OF WALLET

The *product share of wallet* is the most important document you should develop. The more information you have about the clients in a single view, the easier it will become to launch multiple plans of attack. Simply put, the product share of wallet is a tool that will help you target the right customer, at the right time, selling the right product.

Let us assume that you manage eighty accounts. It will be nearly impossible to remember all the opportunities and sales discussions you have ever initiated with clients, unless they are recorded somewhere for later reference. How will you know the next plan of action or the reason for rejection if you don't have the specifics noted down? It is crucial to have all these details available at a single glance for future use.

ADVANCING DEALS IN THE PIPELINE

In sales, the pipeline is the lifeline of the RM. A quick look at the pipeline can indicate whether the RMs will hit their monthly, quarterly, or yearly target.

Managing the pipeline is an art. Only a few salespeople master it. Once the deals are qualified and make their way to the pipeline, it's possible to encounter many challenges along the pipeline stages. If you have been in sales for long enough, you might have realized that the customer will always object or reject your proposition in one form or the other as you move the deal through the pipeline. This is a defining feature of the sales process and will always remain this way.

CLOSING THE DEAL

The last part of the sales framework is Closing the Deal. Unfortunately, many RMs try to get to the closing stage as fast as they can by skipping the earlier stages of the sales framework, only to find themselves crashing into a wall.

Sales takes time. There are no shortcuts. Increasing the probability of closure is only possible when you follow the process properly without skipping stages. Poor discovery and inadequate gap finding are the main reasons for mediocre performance.

The closing stage of the process is a byproduct of how well the previous stages have been handled. The win probability will increase *only* if all stages are managed well.

Chapter 4

WHY DO SALESPEOPLE STRUGGLE?

There are many reasons why salespeople struggle in their careers. Knowing them upfront will save you a lot of trouble down the road. The list below is not comprehensive by any means. I have underlined five broad reasons most relevant to the B2B domain. The good news is that the MST framework shows you how to overcome and address all these shortfalls:

1. No goal/plan
2. Toxic mindset
    a. Lack of discipline
    b. Reactive approach
    c. Giving up from the first "no"
    d. Negative outlook
    e. Poor relationships

f. Not learning or growing
3. Poor sales story
4. Ineffective pipeline management
   a. No constant prospecting
   b. No sales pipeline balance
   c. Stalled deals
   d. Limited product mix
5. Poor targeting

NO GOAL, NO PLAN

It is well known that what is undefined can't be measured, and what is unmeasured cannot be improved. Salespeople fail because they don't have a goal, let alone a plan. Their annual, quarterly, or monthly goals are unclear. I am not talking about the target assigned by the company to its sales force. I am referring to the annual plan that a salesperson intentionally sets for himself.

Do you have an annual plan? If your goal is to hit $1 million in sales by the year's end, what activities will make it possible and by when? Are the activities clearly defined? Can you measure them? Do you have a framework, and are you honoring it? If your answers to these questions are vague, you don't have a plan.

TOXIC SALES MINDSET

A- **Salespeople fail because they lack discipline.** Formulating a decent plan without executing it is as bad as not having one. There is no room in sales for procrastinators.

There are many reasons that could prevent you from carrying out the activities you are supposed to do. You may come to the office tired because you didn't sleep well the night before; as a result, the prospecting for the day gets thrown out the window. Maybe you're having personal issues and don't feel like meeting with clients? Or perhaps you had an accident this morning and didn't feel like meeting with customers? These excuses and many more will pop up every day. What are you going to do? Do you have the discipline to overcome these challenges and stay committed to achieving your goals? Or will you let life get in the way?

B- Salespeople fail because they live in reactive mode. Underperforming salespeople wait for the pipeline to be full, wait for the deal to close, wait for the customer to call them back, and wait for their line manager to teach them a new skill. They wait and continue waiting. Here is a reality check: nothing gets accomplished in a reactive mode. Average salespeople are unproductive simply because they are unsure of what to do when they come to work. Their calendar is empty; as a result, they try to stay busy with whatever comes their way. Before they know it, another day is lost.

C- Salespeople fail because they give up after the first "no." Let me break it to you: no customer on earth will say yes to what you sell after the first round of discussion. The customers will always say no, whether you like it or not, just to protect themselves from the unknowns. However, the word *no* should never discourage you. It is part of sales. It has always been and will continue to be.

D- Salespeople fail because they have a negative outlook. There is no place for negativity in sales. I have never seen negative salespeople hit their quota, but I always see them complain and miss their target miserably. They complain about the target, the clients, their company, and the processes. The list goes on. Don't be surprised if you see them being negative about themselves: "I am too old," "I am too new," "I don't have the courage to do that," "I am not confident to do this". What they fail to realize is that the only problem is their own mindset.

E- Salespeople fail because they don't develop meaningful relationships. The relationship underperforming salespeople have with their clients is superficial; in fact, it doesn't even deserve to be called a relationship. If I only call you for business, it is a business connection; it is never a relationship. Average salespeople fail in developing meaningful relationships because they are not likable. Who likes a person with low EQ, low self-awareness, low self-control, and low social awareness?

F- Salespeople fail because they don't learn and grow. Where do you want to be five years from now? Do you want to stay where you are? Or do you want to grow? No customer wants to do business with a salesperson whose knowledge is below average. What surprises me is that average salespeople don't invest in themselves and still expect to see great results. Imagine if you went to a doctor who stopped learning after graduating twenty years ago. Would you return to this doctor? The answer is a clear no. The same concept applies to salespeople. Don't blame the customers if they don't want to conduct business with you.

POOR SALES STORY

Salespeople fail because they don't have a sales story, let alone a structured one. Having different variations of sales stories for the same products causes them to struggle and become more confused. They can't assess the gap between the current customer's state and the desired future state. They focus more on the product than the customer's preferences.

INEFFECTIVE PIPELINE MANAGEMENT

A- **Salespeople fail because they have an empty pipeline.** They don't proactively schedule time for prospecting and fail to consider it a priority. With no plans for prospecting, they are always desperate to close a deal. More often than not, they find themselves up against the universal law of need: the more desperate you become, the less likely you are to hit your monthly quota.

B- **Salespeople fail because they have an imbalanced pipeline.** Allowing invalid deals to creep into your pipeline is not an effective strategy. The deals in the pipeline have to be managed effectively so they don't stall. A well-balanced pipeline entails a proactive pipeline management approach across all the pipeline stages.

C- **Salespeople fail because of poor pipeline velocity.** They don't put in the effort to advance deals to the next stage. They wait months, if not years, just to realize that the deal is stalled. Their pipeline velocity is below standard, causing pipeline leakage.

D- **Salespeople fail because they don't have a balanced product mix.** They focus on two to three products while ignoring other products, resulting in a loss of numerous business opportunities.

POOR TARGETING

Many salespeople fail because they target the wrong customers. Targeting a market without a strategic plan is not the best approach. The targeted list of customers should be finite. I have yet to see a salesperson who hits his/her quota with a random approach.

EVALUATION AGAINST THE REASONS FOR FAILURE

It is time for reflection. Let's carry out a little activity and identify your areas of weakness so you can address them. Below, score yourself against these five main reasons for failure (on a scale of 1 to 5, where 1 is the issue is not detected, and 5 is the issue is strongly detected).

Toxic mindset

Not Detected				Strongly Detected
1	2	3	4	5

Poor skillset

Not Detected				Strongly Detected
1	2	3	4	5

Ineffective pipeline management

Not Detected				Strongly Detected
1	2	3	4	5

Poor targeting

Not Detected				Strongly Detected
1	2	3	4	5

I suggest that you perform the evaluation once more after you are done reading this book and compare the difference between the two versions. Sometimes we think we know it all, but once we look at ourselves through a new lens, we realize our shortcomings.

The good news is that this book will show you the way. It provides all the solutions to overcome the aforementioned challenges and saves you from falling into any of these traps.

Reach your potential, leverage your capabilities, and pursue the bright future you deserve. Let's crack the sales code.

CRACKING THE SALES CODE

THE SECRET FORMULA TO UNLOCK YOUR SALES POTENTIAL IN BUSINESS SALES

Part II
MINDSET

Chapter 5

SUCCESS BEGINS WITH MINDSET

It has become obvious over the last few years of my sales career that successful salespeople have a growth mindset. Top achievers attribute their success in sales to the mindset they have developed and cherished over time. Nurturing mindset has been one of their obsessions. They realize the importance of managing their outlook, and without it, they are aware that none of the other elements matter. How far can you go with your skillset if you are full of negativity or live in a reactive mode? Not very far.

A *growth mindset* is an intrinsic belief that one can learn with experience and effort. It is the idea that we can approach a situation, challenge the status quo, and think, "What can I do to improve the situation?" The opposite of a growth mindset is a *fixed mindset*, a deep-down belief that people don't change and you are who you are—you are either a top salesperson or you are not, you are either a talented public speaker or you are not meant to be in front of the camera, you either have social skills or you don't have the awareness to deal with people. These two mindset orientations in life have a gigantic impact on how we perform in sales—or in general. Scientists have proven that neurons in our brains continue to develop and grow as we live and breathe. What you can't do becomes a true statement—unless you decide otherwise. As Shakespeare put it, "There is nothing either good or bad but thinking makes it so."

Gerhard Gschwandtner, the author of *Selling Power*, has extensively studied salespeople and their performance. He researched how mindset has a direct correlation to sales results, and suggested that happy salespeople with a strong mindset can sell 38 percent more than average salespeople.

Neuroscience tells us that your inner CEO is located in the prefrontal cortex of your brain. Your inner CEO is in charge of the mindset operating system. If you were to study the brain scans of average salespeople, you would notice that some areas of the brain are not activated. Their minds idle on autopilot mode. They can do a lot more than they are currently doing but fail to realize their potential. Some of the key characteristics of average salespeople are as follows:

- They have control over how their mind operates but do not take advantage of it.
- They have control over how to transform their inner critic to inner champion but do nothing about it.
- They are unfamiliar with the idea that a powerful mindset can help them reach their potential.

Developing and nurturing a sales-driven mindset is crucial to your sales career. No matter how much knowledge and expertise you have in a particular field, without a growth mindset, it is difficult to excel, and you will find yourself readily surrendering to the challenges that get in your way.

GROWTH MINDSET VS. FIXED MINDSET

Carol Dweck, professor of psychology at Stanford University, conducted several studies on how one's mentality influences one's performance. People tend to embrace either a growth mindset or a fixed mindset.

1- Fixed mindset—the belief that you can do little to change your abilities.

2- Growth mindset—the belief that, through effort, you can improve your abilities.

Here is a short quiz to identify what type of mindset you have. Which of the following statements do you think are true?

1- The ability to sell is part of who you are and not something you can change.

2- No matter how good you are at sales, you can always improve.

3- You can learn new selling strategies, but you can't change much about your ability to influence others.

4- Selling is a skill you can develop regardless of your natural talent or personality.

Statements 1 and 3 are *fixed* mindset statements, while statements 2 and 4 are *growth* mindset statements. Do you think the performance of these two groups will be different only because they have different mindsets? You bet. The outcomes these two different groups produce are entirely different. Those with growth mindsets are far more likely to succeed than those with fixed mindsets.

SALES STARTS WITH MINDSET

It all starts with mindset and ends with mindset. Sales involves many challenges that can easily bring your entire career to its knees. The only way to avoid defeat is to embrace a growth sales mindset, which will become your ally on the battlefield. Equipping yourself with a resilient mindset is the right strategy to win the little skirmishes that occur every day in sales.

This piece of the MST framework is crucial, and the responsibility of developing a sales-driven mindset lies completely with you. Do you have a fixed mindset or a growth mindset? If you have a growth mindset, success is the default outcome—enjoy being among the ultra-high performers who overachieve their target every month. If you have a fixed mindset, start reshaping it, and don't let it stop you from achieving your goals. With time and effort, you can transform your fixed mindset into a growth mindset. We will unfold the main elements of a sales-driven mindset in the following chapters.

SIX ELEMENTS OF SALES MINDSET

Mindset comes in many shapes and forms. This book will discuss six major qualities of a sales-driven mindset. There are other qualities not included within the scope of this book that can also impact your sales career, but it is essential to internalize the ones mentioned below first. Focusing primarily on these six elements will help transform your mindset and, eventually, your sales career.

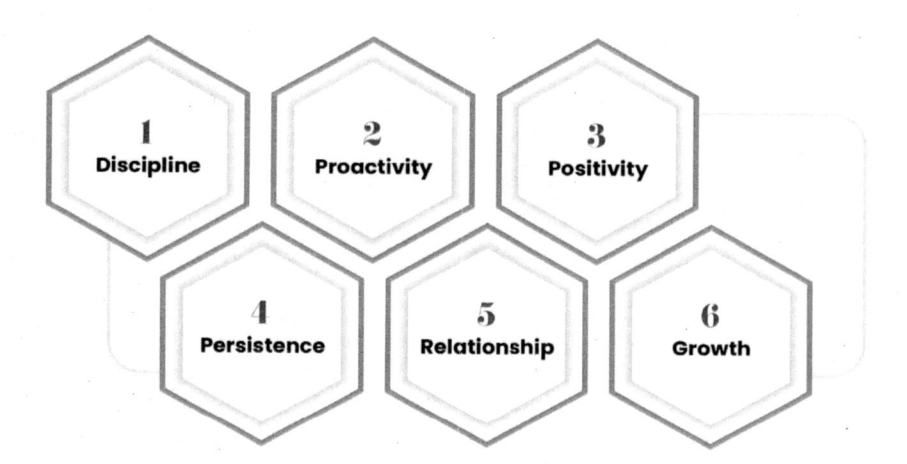

| 1 Discipline | 2 Proactivity | 3 Positivity |
| 4 Persistence | 5 Relationship | 6 Growth |

Chapter 6

MINDSET #1 – DISCIPLINE

Discipline is the bridge between goals and accomplishments.

—Jim Rohn

Self-discipline is a fundamental attribute of all successful sales professionals. Discipline pushes them to act when they do not feel like doing what is required, and even if they don't see immediate results. It gives them the strength to pass up a little pleasure now in exchange for what they really want later. It is necessary to repeat this concept: Disciplined sales professionals are ready to pass up a little pleasure today in exchange for true success tomorrow.

In 1960, Walter Mischel, author of *The Marshmallow Test*, and his colleagues wanted to understand how discipline and self-control influence a successful future. They tested their theory on four-year-old kids by placing a marshmallow in front of them with a promise that if they didn't eat it right away, they would get double the treat when the researcher comes back. The researcher left the room for about fifteen minutes, then returned to see how the children reacted. In the follow-up study, researchers found that children who could wait longer had a better life in the future.

How may the marshmallow test be used in the context of sales? It's simple. The majority of salespeople have instant gratification syndrome and suffer from the affliction of wanting immediate pleasure. They want everything to take place immediately. They want the pipeline to be full now, they want the deal to close now, they want their skills to be at an optimum level now, and they want to build meaningful relationships now. If it is not happening now, they simply give up.

Instant gratification salespeople have a hard time sticking to their plan, and they look for a magic shortcut to success. Salespeople have to learn delayed gratification and demonstrate high self-control, because the reality is that results won't be visible immediately. They need to know that they have to put in consistent work to get results. It could take many months, if not years, to reap the benefits of putting in the hard work today, whether in building the sales pipeline, building meaningful relationships, or enhancing your business acumen.

Meet Andrew, who has recently joined the team as a sales rep in the company. Andrew is enthusiastic about his work and plans to be one of the top producers in his field. After going through the induction program and rigorous product training, he gets a list of accounts to manage. After settling down and building relationships with his accounts, Andrew picks up the phone and manages to build a pipeline through daily prospecting. As you know, the average sales cycle in a company is six to eight months. Here is where Andrew loses his cool, and the desire for instant gratification kicks in. He starts to look for smaller deals to close, because he can't wait for the bigger ones to materialize. Andrew starts to engage in non-sales-related activities, looking for instant gratification—things like engaging in operational activities, meeting his colleagues for a coffee, posting on social media and waiting for a like, and so on. The fact is, Andrew wants everything right now. He's not ready to put in the work today in exchange for a bigger reward in the future. Ultimately, his pipeline shrinks, and before he knows it, he sees his name at the bottom of the performance table and is asked to leave the company. What a sad story. It is a fact that salespeople who don't put in the time and effort now for a bigger reward in the future don't make it, and they will always struggle.

Everything in sales takes time. Mastering your skillset takes time, building meaningful relationships with your clients takes time, creating a pipeline takes time, closing deals takes time—everything around sales takes time. It is wise to learn delayed gratification skills and demonstrate a high level of discipline—to hang in there and ultimately see the success you deserve. Don't eat that marshmallow now. Wait for the double treat in the near future.

Disciplined salespeople do whatever it takes to walk their talk. For instance, if you plan to prospect deals worth $10,000 every day, you will do it, regardless of your circumstances, and you won't get lured away from your goal by instant gratification. Sometimes, you may not feel like calling or are afraid of customers shutting you down. As a result, you don't pick up the phone and dial. However, if you have strong discipline, you will push hard to make that last phone call despite the challenges and boredom. Push yourself to act without an immediate reward. Countless distractions can divert your attention from what you need to do. It takes willpower to ignore them and stick to your work, which may be difficult or boring on a short-term basis but holds a high degree of importance in the long run. For example, conducting two or three productive meetings every day may not bring about an immediate deal closure and is always challenging and hard. However, being disciplined about it will ultimately pay off. Hold yourself accountable for your results and keep the commitments you make.

CREATE A DISCIPLINE LIST

Running a marathon is a goal, but exercising every day is a discipline. Without daily exercise, running a marathon would not be possible. For example, if achieving $10,000 in sales is your target for the month, twenty prospecting calls or three meetings per day should be your daily discipline. Without the daily discipline, achieving the goal will be considerably more difficult.

Develop a list of important activities that will help you achieve your goals. Plan and book them on your calendar. Conducting fifty productive meetings per month may look difficult at the onset, but if you plan two or three meetings per day, achieving the number is easy. Here are examples of some of the important activities that you can book on your calendar. Meet with your line manager and decide the right number for yourself.

- Make twenty prospecting phone calls every day.
- Schedule two physical meetings every day.
- Schedule two virtual meetings every day.
- Move five leads from targeted to active stage every week. (Advancing deals from one stage to another will be discussed in part 3 of the book).

- Move five leads from active to hot stage every week.
- Move three leads from hot to closed stage every week.
- Analyze product balance every week.
- Schedule forty-five minutes on enhancing product knowledge every day.
- Read ten pages of any business book every day.
- Build meaningful relationships with your clients every day.
- Connect with four CEOs every week.

Focus on one activity at a time; multitasking seldom works. If you plan to advance the deals in the pipeline within the next hour, this should be your only focus. Don't look at your email or your phone. Let your team lead and peers know that you are busy now, and you will get back to them when you are done.

DISCIPLINE BREEDS CONSISTENCY

Discipline paves the way for consistency. Only disciplined salespeople will do what it takes to succeed consistently. They are not distracted by unimportant things and remain focused on what matters most.

Success in sales ultimately comes down to how often we do the little things. It is not about closing a big deal now and then; it's about doing the little things on a consistent basis.

Average salespeople are easily distracted and quickly fall back to their old way of doing things. They stop doing what is required and put it off for later. Not being consistent is an obvious issue, but we refuse to do something about it.

Doing the same thing over and over again leads to boredom. What do successful people do that others don't? Successful salespeople are in love with boredom. Interesting work undoubtedly captivates us, but more often than not, we tend to shy away from the boring stuff. In sales, it all comes down to who can handle the boredom. Top performers feel the same lack of motivation as everyone else, but the difference is that they find a way to show up despite the feeling of boredom. Mastery requires practice, but the more you practice something, the more boring it becomes.

The greatest threat to success is boredom. As we get used to all the activities that are repeated daily in sales, we seek novelty and let go of the most important tasks that we can't succeed without, even if the shiny new thing doesn't add any value to our sales career.

Everyone faces the same challenge on their journey to success in sales. If you only do the work when it is convenient or exciting, you will not be consistent enough to achieve remarkable results. Obviously, when you start to do the little things every day, you will feel like quitting. When it is time to prospect, there will be days when you don't feel like picking up the phone. When it is time to enhance your skillset, there will be days when you don't feel like reading. When it is time to book your calendar, there will be days when you don't feel like scheduling your meetings. However, stepping up when it is annoying, exhausting, demotivating—that is the difference between a sales professional and an underperformer. Top producers stick to the schedule, while mediocre ones let things get in the way. Top producers know what is important to them and keep doing it despite the boredom. On the other hand, mediocre ones get pulled away by unrelated sales activities.

Success in life doesn't happen overnight. To be in the elite category, you need to engage in an activity a thousand times. Think about a musician who plays a piano. How many times did he or she practice to achieve perfection? Think about a football player. How many times did he or she train to master his game? Think about an artist. How many times did he or she paint to create a masterpiece of art? Here is a question for you: How many times have you tried to master your craft in sales? In the last year, how many calls have you made? How many meetings have you done? How many books have you read? How many meaningful relationships have you built?

Great things and mastery can be achieved when we do the important things on a consistent basis. Similar to compound interest, sales activities compound. Read two books a month and you will finish twenty-four books in a year. Listen to two audiobooks a month and you will finish twenty-four audiobooks in a year. Enroll in a course each month, and you will complete twelve courses in a year. Meet with three customers per day and you will end up meeting 860 times per year. Call ten customers per day and you will end up making 2,800 productive sales calls per year. Only elite sales professionals understand the power of consistency, and they don't let anything come in the way of being successful. Make a plan and stick to it. Let the most crucial thing in your life and career compound.

DISCIPLINE BREEDS COMMITMENT

Grant Cardone, author of *Sell or Be Sold*, says committing to the wrong thing all the way is better than committing to the right thing halfway. Commit all the way and burn all the bridges—leave no alternatives. Eliminate your options and learn everything you can about selling and about your job.

Taking extreme ownership of everything in your life is your responsibility. Taking extreme ownership will make you reach your potential and beyond.

Commit and take ownership of the following aspects in your sales career:

- Commit to believing in yourself.
- Commit to your company.
- Commit to your target.
- Commit to learning everything about sales.
- Commit to developing your mindset.
- Commit to developing your skillset.
- Commit to building meaningful relationships with your customers.
- Commit to learning about the products and solutions.
- Commit to prospecting every day.
- Commit to advancing the deals in the pipeline every day.
- Commit, commit, and commit if you want to succeed in your career.

COMMITMENT NEEDS CLARITY

Goals can be achieved and dreams can be fulfilled when you put your commitment in writing. Writing your goals is a compelling exercise because of the clarity you will achieve regarding the what, when, and where. Clarity leads to a strong commitment and increases the likelihood of plan execution.

James Clear shares an interesting study on how to build better habits in his book *Atomic Habits*. A group of researchers in the UK worked with 248 people to understand how to build better exercise habits. The researchers divided the participants into three groups.

The first group was the control group; they were asked to simply track their numbers. The second group was the motivation group. They were told to read some material on the benefits of exercise on overall health. In addition, the researchers delivered a motivational presentation to encourage the group to make exercise a daily habit. The last group was the clarity group. They were told to formulate a plan for when and where to exercise over the next two weeks. They were asked to complete the following sentence: "During the following weeks, I will exercise for twenty minutes on this day_____ at this time_____ in this place_____."

In the first two groups, 35 to 38 percent exercised at least once a week. Interestingly, the motivational talk delivered to the motivation group didn't impact them much. However, 91 percent of the people in the third group exercised at least once per week—more than double the rate. The sentence they filled out is what the researchers referred to as *implementation intention*, which indicates what, when, and where to execute the plan. The conclusion is that the first two groups didn't lack motivation. What they actually lacked was *clarity*.

In a similar context, if you formulate a plan that says, "I will meet three customers per day at their location to sell digital solutions, one meeting is at 10:00, the second meeting is at 12:00, and the last meeting is at 2:00," there is a high likelihood that you will execute the plan, simply because you have more clarity on the specifics of the activity.

In addition to clarity, sharing your commitment in public is a great strategy to hold yourself accountable to the plan. If you are like most people, you care about what others think of you. Making the commitment in public will push you to try harder to honor it and motivate you to become more self-disciplined.

Share your plan with your colleagues—for example, the size of the pipeline you plan to build, the number of meetings you'd like to schedule in a month, or the type of relationships you want to have with your clients.

MULTILEVEL GOALS

Dr. Covey, author of *The Seven Habits of Highly Effective People*, suggested that everything is created twice: once when you plan and once when you execute. Proactive salespeople take the time to set priorities and challenging goals that will keep them motivated and focused throughout the year. Everything they do is ultimately linked to the final goal. A salesperson without a goal is like a ship without a compass, sailing in the sea, not knowing where to go. If you don't have a figure in mind, where do you think you are headed? How will you evaluate yourself by the end of the month, quarter, or year? How will you celebrate, and on what basis?

Setting the right goals is both an art and a science. If your goals are too easy, your performance won't improve. If they are too stretched, you won't even attempt to hit them. Targets must be attainable and within reach. In addition, targets should be measurable. If you state that you want to increase revenue, then this statement is not a target; it's just a wish list. In addition to being clear, attainable, and measurable, targets should be stamped with a timeframe. Targets should not be left open-ended. Here is an example of a good target statement: You could say that your goal is to increase revenue by 4 percent by the end of December.

Goal setting is an activity that many salespeople try to avoid, simply because they are afraid of failing. There is nothing wrong with failing. The more you fail, the more you learn. The more you learn, the easier it is to achieve your goal. As Edison said, "I have not failed, I just found a thousand ways that don't work."

Goal setting can be for one year, two years, five years, or maybe ten years. Where do you want to be ten years from now? Is what you are doing now bringing you closer to your goals? It's never too late to reflect on your own performance—act now.

Jason Jordon, author of *Cracking the Sales Management Code*, suggests that the ultimate goals can't be managed directly. In order to reach business results, i.e., revenue, the sales objectives need to be managed, and in order to manage the sales objectives, sales activities need to be managed. Therefore, the sales activities drive the sales objectives, and the sales objectives influence the business results.

On the same note, Angela Duckworth, author of *Grit*, shows how to set high-level, mid-level, and low-level goals. Low-level goals drive mid-level goals, and mid-level goals ultimately drive high-level goals. It is never the other way around—you can't manage the high-level goals directly without managing the mid-level and low-level goals. Let's look at how both concepts integrate to set the right goals and objectives.

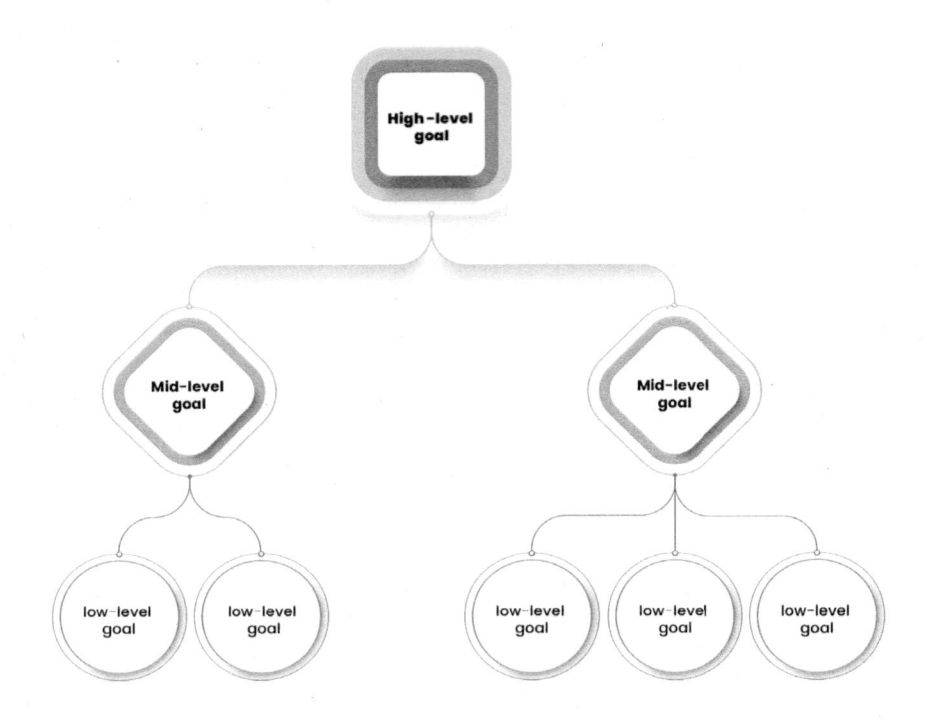

Goals Structure

HIGH-LEVEL GOALS

High-level goals are generally the purpose of the existence of the business. They typically fall under three broad categories:

- Financial results
- Customer satisfaction results
- Market share results

High-level goals are goals that you have always dreamt of achieving. Every decision you make in your career should be aligned with the top-level goals. Star players know that high-level goals aim to grow revenue, enhance customer satisfaction, and gain market share.

In the words of Lord Kelvin, a physicist and mathematician, "What is not defined, cannot be measured. What is not measured, cannot be improved. What is not improved, is always degraded." High-level goals should be measurable in order to track progress toward them. If you say, "I plan to increase revenue," decide by how much and by when. It should go something like this: "By the end of the year, I plan to increase revenue by 5 percent." Similarly, if you plan to enhance customer satisfaction, you could say, "By the end of the year, my goal is to enhance customer satisfaction by 10 percent," and so on.

Can these high-level goals be managed? Can you say, "I plan to grow revenue," and do nothing about it? Of course not. This is where the mid-level goals come into play.

MID-LEVEL GOALS

Mid-level goals are the sales objectives you aspire to fulfill between one month and six months. Unlike high-level goals, mid-level goals are dynamic and can be adjusted in a way that supports your top-level goals. They include market coverage, building capabilities, customer focus, and product focus. These sales objectives will ultimately drive the top-level goals. Tackling market coverage will, in turn, influence high-level goals. The same holds true for building capabilities: When you get equipped with the right skills, you will affect the high-level goals. The impact on business results will be even greater if you intentionally plan your activities to focus on the right customers and strategize around the right product for a particular market.

Setting a clear target across these objectives to influence high-level goals is imperative; otherwise, the plan will be vague, and doors for excuses will blow wide open. Here is an example of how to set a target across these sales objectives:

- Market coverage:
    - Meet with my clients at least once a month.
    - Replace growing accounts with declining ones.
- Building capabilities:
    - Enhance product knowledge on ten products this year.
    - Attend twenty courses per year.
    - Get certified in cloud and security by year-end.
    - Read ten sales books by November.
- Customer focus:
    - Build meaningful relationships with the customers by conducting fifty meetings per month.
    - Meet ten C-level executives per month.
    - Connect with thirty customers this year over LinkedIn.
- Product focus:
    - Focus on the cloud in the next three months.
    - Attack retail IoT this month.
    - Generate $30,000 in value from the cloud in the next six months.
    - Sell twenty security products in the next six months.

LOW-LEVEL GOALS

Low-level goals are the activities that drive the sales objectives, which are mid-level goals. For instance, if the sales objective is to hit $100,000 per month, what should be your activity-level target? These are the daily or weekly disciplines you should carry out to ultimately achieve your top-level goals. For example:

- Call management:
    - Make twenty prospecting phone calls per day.
    - Do pre-call planning one day before.
    - Visit three customers per day.
- Opportunity management:
    - Create seven opportunities every week.
    - Move ten deals from targeted to active stage every week.
    - Advance six opportunities from active to hot stage every week.
    - Advance two opportunities from hot to closed stage every week.
- Relationship management:
    - Visit three customers per day.
    - Take three customers to lunch every month.
    - Invite two customers to a roundtable discussion every week.
- Territory management:
    - Meet the growing accounts once a week.
    - Meet the non-growing accounts once a month.
- Sales force skillset:
    - Craft my sales story around a particular product once a week.

- o Read a sales book every two weeks.
- o Do extensive learning on one product per week.

For low-level goals to get accomplished, they have to be booked on your calendar at least a week in advance. Low-level goals are dynamic and can change depending on the situation. All of these low-level goals are part of the Schedule quadrant (more details on the Schedule quadrant in the next chapter). You won't get them done without proper planning.

TRACKING YOUR PROGRESS

Setting a goal can be one thing, but reviewing it on a consistent basis is another. Richard Branson believes that millionaires read their goals one to seventeen times a day. He reads his goals twenty-one times each day. A study found that if people read their goals once a week, they achieve four to six goals out of ten during the course of the year. However, if they read their goals once a day, they are likely to achieve seven to nine out of ten goals during the course of a year.

To achieve remarkable performance in sales, setting goals is not enough. It is equally important to evaluate, measure, monitor, and enhance these goals on a recurring basis. Monitoring performance provides an early warning of potential problems and allows you to make adjustments in order to keep your performance on track. Tracking your performance will make sense if the target is clear, simple, measurable, attainable, and time bound. Vague and unrealistic goals will demotivate you, and the likelihood of chasing them will dwindle.

SELF-ACCOUNTABILITY

Performance monitoring is a systematic and periodic observation of performance over time in order to develop and uncover performance gaps before they become unmanageable. Paying close attention to the performance dashboard and, most importantly, holding yourself accountable for the numbers are important drivers for exceptional performance. When we look at our numbers, we recognize that we have a problem in a specific area. But we often refuse to do anything about it because taking action is hard, being proactive is hard, and being responsible for our numbers is hard. Don't let complacency get in the way. You know exactly what to do to be successful. Take extreme ownership and devise a plan of action to put things back on track.

ONE-ON-ONE COACHING SESSION

Keith Rosen, author of *Sales Leadership*, defines *coaching* as "an art of co-creating new possibilities." Every great athlete has a coach, and so does a great sales professional. Why do athletes need coaches when they always beat their coaches in their domain? Why does Ronaldo, Serena Williams, or Usain Bolt need a coach? A coach plays an integral part in the success of our lives. Working with a coach creates new possibilities that never existed before.

In sales, we all need coaches, because a coach pushes us beyond our limits and ensures that we reach our potential. Sometimes, we take a back seat and don't put in the time and effort to advance our performance. When things go sideways, we need someone to put us back on track. When we lack motivation, we need someone to remind us of our ultimate goals. When things get in the way, we need someone to support our mission. The role of a coach is critical. You need a partner to help you address these challenges and help achieve 200 percent of your capabilities.

Scheduling a regular one-on-one session with your line manager is very important. Having someone hold you responsible for your high-level, mid-level, and low-level goals is fundamental for your success in sales.

Coaching happens, either on the spot or as a structured one-on-one meeting with your line manager or someone else you think will be a great coach. While on-the-spot coaching will take place whenever the situation demands, structured coaching requires alignment between you and the coach. Go ahead and have a conversation with your coach and set clear expectations. If the sales culture you work in encourages coaching, utilize it to your advantage. If it doesn't, do it by yourself. Schedule one-on-one sessions with your coach and agree on a format that works best for both of you.

Decide how often these coaching sessions should take place. Having weekly sessions is the ideal model for the best results. Here are examples of what to discuss in these types of sessions:

- Review past and current performance, and plan for future performance.
- Review high-level goals.
- Review mid-level goals.
- Review low-level goals.
- Evaluate if these goals are relevant and current.
- Review your pipeline.
- Review your calendar.
- Review your skillset development plan.
- Review engagement with the clients.
- Review challenges and needed support.

- Review commitment around numbers for next week.
- List top key activities to engage in next week.
- Decide on clear next steps and clear next coaching session date.

A sample of a coaching form is in the appendix of the book.

MY MARATHON STORY

When I started long-distance running in March 2019, I set a challenging high-level goal of running a 42.2 km marathon in August 2020. At the time, all I could run was 6 km, and running a marathon was only a dream. When I shared my top-level goal with my coach, he immediately said, "Hassan, I can see you crossing the finish line and celebrating your success. Nothing can stop you from attaining your goal except yourself and your mindset."

Then I asked myself, what does it take to achieve the goal? I started to plan the mid-level goals, which were running 10 km by March 2020, 20 km by May 2020, and 30 km by July 2020. I assume you've learned that mid-level goals can't be managed unless you go one level lower. Things get tough and challenging, and this is where your mindset becomes either your ally or adversary. Achieving low-level goals is challenging. You will feel bored, tired, and demotivated; however, you need to be disciplined, proactive, persistent, and positive, despite the setbacks. I worked with my coach and laid clear and measurable low-level goals:

- Watch my diet every day.
- Sleep well every day.
- Train four times a week.

- Conduct interval training once a week – 5 km.
- Incorporate speed work once a week – 5 km.
- Do a slow running routine once a week – 5 km.
- Do long-distance running once a week at an increment of 2 km per week.

When I put the plan into action, the first 7 km was incredibly hard on my legs and knees, as I was unaccustomed to long-distance running. But I was disciplined about my low-level goals. I incorporated all the activities into my weekly routine and followed the plan. Because of my low-level goals, despite the COVID-19 pandemic, which forced lockdowns, social distancing, and gym closures, I was able to continue with my training. It would have been an easy excuse to stop running. But commitment and extreme ownership are what separate the achievers from the naysayers.

Then, I gradually built it up to 12 km, 14 km, 16 km, 18 km, and 21 km. Just think for a moment: If I hadn't taken the time to set goals at these three levels, would I have pressed on to reach 21 km? I don't think so.

After hitting the first target of 21 km, I knew that I could break the 30 km barrier, but I had to stay disciplined and put in constant effort. By training on a weekly basis and having a regular performance review with my coach, I was able to run increasing distances of 24 km, 26 km, 28 km, and 32 km. On August 2, 2020, I ran a full marathon of 42.2 km. It was an amazing feeling of accomplishment that no words can describe.

I am not sure if running a marathon would have been possible without setting a goal in my mind, because it was the only source of encouragement to wake up in the morning and run. If you do not set a challenging goal to work toward in your career and don't have a coach who will hold you responsible for your activities, what do you think will keep you motivated?

Chapter 7

MINDSET #2 – PROACTIVITY

Newton's first law of motion says that an object at rest tends to remain at rest, and an object in motion remains in motion, unless it is acted upon by an external force. In other words, the status quo prevails unless you decide to change it.

The proactivity chapter is inspired by one of the most influential books of all time: *The Seven Habits of Highly Effective People* by Dr. Steven R. Covey. This book had a huge impact on my life and career. Dr. Covey said that between stimulus and response lies our freedom to choose, a very powerful statement that suggests we have the power to choose how to respond to our circumstances. While we do not have control over what happens to us, we definitely have control over how we react. In sales, many things are out of our control, and how we tackle them is entirely up to us.

The difference between salespeople who are proactive and those who are not is the difference between success and failure. It is not a 20 to 50 percent difference in effectiveness. It's about a 5,000 percent difference, especially if the salesperson is smart and aware.

Reactive salespeople are often affected by the environment around them. Proactive salespeople build their own environment. They choose to take action to enhance their lives and never wait to be acted upon. They take charge of their own success in sales. They do not wait for other people to teach them or tell them what to do and how to do it.

Unfortunately, average salespeople fail because they wait for things to happen to them. They wait for their line manager to tell them what to do, they wait to be enrolled in a training course, they wait to be told which product they should enhance their skills on, they wait for the customer to call, they wait for their sales managers to push them to schedule meetings for next week, they wait for the opportunity to pop up, they wait and achieve nothing through the constant wait—just writing this sentence made me feel nauseated. Unfortunately, many are just like that. They complain and blame everything around them except themselves.

BE PROACTIVE TO BE PRODUCTIVE

	1 DO FIRST Important and urgent	2 SCHEDULE Important, not urgent
	3 DELEGATE Not important, urgent	4 DELETE Not important, nor urgent

Eisenhower Matrix

The Eisenhower matrix is a proactivity tool that enables sales professionals to achieve more with fewer resources. As you know, not all tasks are important. Some tasks deliver substantial outcomes, while others are just a waste of time. Salespeople often get caught up in activities that are neither urgent nor important. Focusing on nonproductive tasks is the main reason mediocre salespeople fail. On the other hand, proactive sales professionals understand that time is precious; they do whatever it takes to protect it and expend it wisely.

1. Do First Quadrant—Important and Urgent

There are two types of urgent and important tasks: unforeseen activities and activities that have been delayed until the last minute. For the activities that are unforeseen, you can always leave white spaces on your calendar to tackle them when they arise. These are things like service disruption, accidents, critical customer issues, and so on. However, the last-minute activities can be avoided by planning in advance. The activities that fall under quadrants 2 or 3 become important and urgent at some point in time if you don't proactively get them done. For example, if you don't book the prospecting task on your calendar every day, you will end up with an empty pipeline. As a result, you will become desperate, and prospecting will become an urgent and important activity. The cycle of firefighting will start, the stress will build up, and the struggling salesperson will feel overwhelmed with so many tasks that they could have avoided in the first place. Fix the Schedule quadrant, and everything else will fall into place.

2. Schedule Quadrant—Important but Not Urgent

These are tasks that are important but not urgent at the moment because there is no firm deadline yet. Proactive salespeople set aside time and ensure that most of their time is dedicated to the tasks that fall under the Schedule quadrant. If you don't intentionally book these tasks on your calendar, your time will be spent on firefighting activities that are neither important nor urgent. Since the tasks in the schedule quadrant are not urgent, they don't demand your time immediately. However, these activities are extremely important for your life and career. Ultra-high performers know this and live by it. Nothing can distract them from carrying out the activities that may not be urgent, but still hold an enormous degree of importance.

Set a deadline for these important tasks and book them in your calendar—if there is no deadline, nothing gets accomplished. Here are some of the tasks that may not be urgent, but still have an overall impact on your career: building meaningful relationships, reading a sales book, attending a product training, learning about a new technology, sharpening your sales story, prospecting, managing your pipeline, etc.

3. Delegate Quadrant—Not Important but Urgent

These tasks are unimportant but seemingly urgent; they are best described as *busywork*. Many salespeople want to be busy, because scheduling an important activity seems to be difficult and requires proactivity on their part. As a result, they tend to spend time doing tasks that are not important just because they are easy and simple to do. Being busy doesn't mean that you are productive, and unimportant activities will not get you closer to your goals. Identify these activities and delegate them to someone else—things like filling an Excel sheet, delivering a package, logging an activity in the system, engaging in operational activities, and so on. Do yourself a favor—delegate these tasks and focus your time on the activities that fall under the Schedule quadrant.

4. Delete Quadrant—Not Important nor Urgent

And here comes the Dracula of time: tasks that are neither important nor urgent. Proactive salespeople understand the importance of time and never engage in time-wasting activities. Unfortunately, this is where underperformance dwells. Mediocre salespeople continue to engage in these activities and don't know that these tasks will derail their careers. Identify these activities and cut them out of your day. Here are a few examples of time-sucking activities: social media, watching TV, chatting with friends, playing video games, and so on. I feel bad for people who get stuck wasting their time on these activities. They want to be on top, but the reality on the ground is different. Check what the activities in the Schedule quadrant are and focus your time and energy there.

WHAT DOES YOUR CALENDAR LOOK LIKE?

Show me your calendar, and I will tell you with 95 percent accuracy whether you are a proactive and productive salesperson. We have all attended time-management courses or heard about time management from a friend. Even though time management seems to be a simple skill that everyone can master, only a few relationship managers are able to manage their time in a productive way.

We read in the beginning of the book about how Ahmed was struggling with sales, and one of the reasons was he was not paying attention to this simple but powerful tool that can help increase his productivity exponentially. Ahmed came to work not knowing what to do and started to engage in non-related sales activities just to look busy. Before he knew it, the day was over. There were no sales meetings, no prospecting, and no achievements. Another precious day was wasted.

Successful salespeople take a different approach to managing their day. If you take a look at their calendars, you will see the week filled with sales-related activities like prospecting, meeting with customers virtually, meeting with customers physically, learning, and developing. They've also allocated white space for urgent matters. They are engaged with the Schedule quadrant activities that they know will ultimately pay off.

Let's look at a productive salesperson's calendar and see what it looks like:

	TUESDAY	WEDNESDAY	THURSDAY
06:00AM	Hit The Gym	Hit The Gym	Read A Sales Book
07:00AM			
08:00AM	Read A Sales Book	Morning Huddle	White Space
09:00AM	Coaching Session	Meeting With AKR	Meeting With KKR
10:00AM	Meeting With ABBR	White Space	Meeting With CEO Of MMD
11:00AM	Meeting With RCB	Meeting With MRK	Meeting With CEO Of MMD
12:00PM	White Space	HOD Meeting	Meeting With CEO Of MMD
01:00PM	White Space	HOD Meeting	White Space
02:00PM	Meeting With RCA	White Space	Operation Meeting
03:00PM	Meeting With RCA	Meeting With RCA	Operation Meeting
04:00PM		Meeting With RCA	
05:00PM	Clear Emails	Clear Emails	Clear Emails
06:00PM			

Top performers do the most important things at the start of their day. With a fresh mind in the morning, they spend their time and energy on activities that contribute to their development, personally and professionally. Notice from the calendar that a few items are repeated every day or on alternate days without fail, for example:

1- Physical fitness
2- Self-development
3- Prospecting
4- Pipeline balancing
5- Meeting customers virtually
6- Meeting customers face-to-face
7- Reading emails and solving problems

Doing the first things first is evident on the calendar. Unproductive salespeople engage in the least important things first. Do you really want to read emails with a fresh mind in the morning? Or would you rather read a sales book? Or engage in a brainstorming activity with your colleagues to enhance a business process or solve a business problem?

Notice that there are also white spaces on the calendar that account for unplanned and urgent events. These free spaces on your calendar are necessary, as sometimes your day won't go as planned. But if you stick to your plan 80 to 90 percent of the time, you are on your way to a successful life and career. The proactive and productive activities we do every day are not noticeable in the short run but will definitely have a tremendous impact in the long run.

Time is perishable. Spend it wisely. Proactive salespeople take control of their calendar and plan at least seven days ahead. Smart salespeople know that if they schedule seven days ahead, other people's calendars will be empty, so they can place their meetings on the prospect's calendar on the date and time they want. They also know that what's not booked on the calendar won't get accomplished. Don't assume that customers have nothing to do but wait for your call. People are busy the same way you are, so respect their time and yours. Sometimes, you can get away with calling the customers without a plan to pitch a product, but it is not an effective strategy. Schedule it on your calendar!

PROACTIVE SALESPEOPLE TAKE MASSIVE ACTION

When I started reading sales books, one of the early books I picked up was *Sell or Be Sold* by Grant Cardone. Grant shares his personal experience and how he progressed from a normal guy to a professional sales consultant. In his book, he talked about the "massive action" concept. This concept has affected me so much that I would not have been in this role in SMB if I had not taken massive action.

I am accustomed to performing a weekly brainstorming session, early in the morning, with myself; it is booked on my calendar so I don't forget. Before starting the session, I write "massive action" on top of the page. I know for a fact that every beautiful thing in life that you and I appreciate didn't come from normal action. Someone, somewhere, took massive action to make it happen. Me writing this each day is a reminder to myself to take massive action if I want to progress from good to great.

If transforming your sales career from good to great is something you also aspire to fulfill, take massive action. Be crazy about the level of activity you do. If your line manager asks you to make twenty prospecting phone calls per day, make forty or fifty calls—this is massive action. Don't settle for mediocrity; go all out and do more than what is required.

On the other hand, reactive salespeople take action when they are unable to hit their target and find themselves with an empty pipeline. Desperation kicks in, and their line manager threatens to put them on a performance-improvement plan. They are unable to accomplish anything because they did not take any action, let alone massive action.

Ultra-high performers understand the importance of massive action. They do what it takes and more because it is in their DNA. So if you want to be among the top performers, forget about the mediocre normal action and start planning for massive action.

Chapter 8

MINDSET #3 – POSITIVITY

Roger Bannister made headlines around the world by being the first person to break a mile in under four minutes in 1954. Up until that time, no one thought breaking a sub-four-minute mile was possible. The interesting thing is that Bannister's record was broken forty-six days later by another runner. Since that time, a thousand athletes have crossed the four-minute mile. What has changed? Why is a sub-four-minute mile easy to accomplish all of a sudden? The only thing that changed is the negative self-talk surrounding this goal. People changed their beliefs and started to say, "If he could do it, I can too."

Maybe you are not running a sub-four-minute mile or a marathon, but you are definitely planning on running a better sales race. Any negative self-talk will greatly impact the way you perform.

To succeed in sales, you must either have or develop optimism. Research shows that optimistic salespeople outsell their pessimistic peers by 88 percent. I have seen many optimistic relationship managers meet their numbers consistently, but I have yet to see any pessimistic salesperson achieve their target; they just don't exist.

Optimism nurtures initiative. On the other hand, pessimism kills initiative. Optimism keeps you going, while pessimism makes you stop. It is the difference between life and death, and in sales, there is no room for dead people. They may exist in other departments, but not in sales.

IDENTIFY YOUR SELF-LIMITING BELIEF

According to research from Harvard Business School, just saying the words, "I am excited," in a high-pressure situation is proven to relieve stress and instill self-confidence, leading to better performance.

Self-limiting beliefs are formed by repeating negative self-talk. Try to repeat something to yourself over and over again, and you have no choice but to believe it, whether it is right or wrong. Try to say that it is hard to sell cloud solutions, and you have no choice but to endorse it. Watch out for all self-limiting beliefs about yourself, your company, and your products. Remember, what you are not aware of, you cannot change. What you are not aware of, you are bound to repeat. Pay attention when negativity creeps in, and dismiss it immediately.

Have you ever said any of these statements to yourself or to someone else?

- I have tried many times, but I feel I am just not good at it.
- I don't know how to pitch this product; it is too hard.
- This product sucks. Nobody will buy it.
- The economy isn't good. No one is buying right now.
- I have tier-three accounts; in fact, all of my tier-one accounts are bad.

Mindset #3 – Positivity

- I tried many times, and no one wants to buy anything.
- My team lead prevents me from succeeding and keeps micromanaging me.
- The competitors always beat me on price. I lost a couple of deals just because of that.
- The support is not so good. I lost many deals because of the delay in submitting the proposals.
- I am not trained well to do my job in the right way.
- I am too young to call on the C-level executives.
- All decision-makers are busy, and it is hard to meet with them.
- There is no reason for the customer to buy.
- I will just do my job.

These excuses allow pessimism to destroy your career. Even if some of these statements are true, you are allowing pessimism to guide your thoughts. Don't let pessimism find its way to you.

Be enthusiastic and optimistic and hope for a better future. Be convinced that good things will happen even if there is no evidence in the initial stages. Be optimistic, envision success, and develop the belief that you can make a difference. Your success depends on the belief that the solution will add value to the customer, even if the customer does not realize it from the first round of discussion.

The more you believe in yourself and your success, the more motivated you will be to achieve it. If you expect success, you will do whatever it takes to succeed. On the other hand, if you expect failure, you can't help but act in a way that ensures it.

WITH OPTIMISM COMES PRODUCT BELIEF

The degree to which you are sold on the product you sell determines the degree to which you will be successful. Believing that the product you sell is superior to all other products available on the market is the first step toward top performance. You have to be convinced that there is no other product in the market that matches the superiority of your product. Sell it to yourself before selling it to others and believe with 100 percent certainty that your product or solution will solve the problem of your customer or will help them achieve great results or capture an opportunity in the near future.

The moment doubts about your product or company creep into your mind, you will begin to struggle and limit your ability to sell. As a result, your confidence level will drop. Dare to think that there are better products in the market, and you are doomed to fail. If you think there are other products with the same quality as your products but with a lower price, you will get nothing but failure. If you think you will not be able to sell the product—for any reason—you will fail!

Expel all the negativity and be certain, without a doubt, that your product is absolutely the best in the market and that you are doing the customer a favor by selling it to them. There is no other way to succeed. Believe in yourself, believe in your product, and believe in your company.

CAMPING ZONE

Meet Sandeep, who has been an inconsistent performer over the past few months. His performance was not up to expectations, and he has been struggling for some time. He missed the current quarter's target and the previous quarter's target. His sales pipeline is empty, and there is no sign that things will get better in the future. In my review with Sandeep, here is how the conversation went:

Me: Sandeep, looking at the numbers, I get the feeling that you need help. Is everything okay?

Sandeep: Yeah, it has been a challenging month.

Me: What I want is for you to be a consistent performer and achieve the target every month and have fun at the same time. I can see that you missed last quarter's target—is there anything we should know? Do you need any support? I see no opportunities created the last month. I would like to work with you to understand all the challenges and build a solid plan to fix the current situation. Are you open to that?

Sandeep: Yes, I am open. In fact, I am trying very hard to create new opportunities, but most of my accounts are headquartered in other countries. They only have a small representative office here in Dubai, so I can't sell them anything, as the decision-makers are not reachable. The remaining accounts I have are dead. They don't want to meet, and they don't want to buy.

Me: How do you usually manage your day?

Sandeep: I am also unable to find time. I report to work at seven. I start to work on my emails and handle all the operational tasks to ensure my customers get the best service. I usually try to pick up the phone and call the customers at ten, and if they are ready to meet, I drive to their office and meet with them. I talk about all the products to ensure the customer knows about our product portfolio and reaches out to us when new requirements pop up.

Me: Sounds good. Sandeep, there are a few observations that I have. Let's work together to address them.

How many issues can you detect in Sandeep's approach? Can you highlight the main problems and the underlying causes? Take a moment to read the above scenario again and think before reading my observations.

Observations:

The effect: an empty pipeline that led to underperformance for the last two quarters. What is the root cause that led to the empty pipeline? There are many; let's discuss them.

1- Negativity: Sandeep doesn't think he can sell to these types of customers, creating the very problem he wants to avoid. When negativity enters the mind, there is no choice but to believe it. Therefore, you stop approaching any customer because of the belief that they are dead, which may not be true. These are just assumptions made up in the subconscious mind. The reality is that Sandeep is dead!

2- No meaningful relationships with the accounts. Sandeep is anchored to one stakeholder in the company and doesn't make an effort to level up to the decision-makers. You know that nothing happens at the ground level. All the decisions are made at the C-level. If you are not in contact with the C-level executives, don't expect deals to find their way to you.

3- Nonproductive day because of the timing gap. Sandeep reports to work at seven, while the stakeholders in the companies he manages report to work at nine. There is a clear timing gap between him and his clients. It is evident that Sandeep always seems to be pressed for time and unable to meet with his clients regularly.

4- Empty calendar. Sandeep doesn't seem to have control of his calendar; he lives in a reactive mode. No meetings are booked—he just tries to stay busy and does the best he can.

5- Operation focus. Sandeep spends three hours checking emails and being busy with operational activities, when his primary job is to focus on sales activities.

6- Random approach to market. Sandeep doesn't have a clear go-to-market strategy and tries to sell all products without putting in the effort to understand the customer first.

It is no surprise that Sandeep does not meet his target. In the first few minutes with him, we have uncovered these six problems. Do you think Sandeep is optimistic about the future of his sales career? Will he succeed if he doesn't address all of these issues? Is he aware that these problems exist in the first place? I don't think so. It is unfortunate that average relationship managers who want to be top performers create the problems they are trying to avoid. That which you are not aware of, you cannot change. That which you are not aware of, you are bound to repeat. That's it.

Chapter 9

MINDSET #4 – PERSISTENCE

Persistence or *perseverance* is the act of selecting a desired outcome and sticking to it until you achieve it. Persistence is an integral part of succeeding in sales. Without it, you will definitely struggle. Here is a little piece of advice though: No customer on earth will agree to buy your solution from the first round of discussion. Their first response to your pitch, quotation, or proposal will invariably be a no. Don't be disheartened—this is normal, and it will always be this way for as long as you are in sales, and even after.

When I ask relationship managers what the golden rule of sales is, 90 percent of the time, the answer is: "The customer is always right." While I am not saying that we should treat the customers unfairly, that answer is incorrect. The golden rule of sales is, "The customer will always say no." If you plan to pursue a career in sales, you should learn to accept that reality.

"NO" DOES NOT MEAN NEVER; IT MEANS "NOT YET"

"The success is on the far side of the failure," said IBM founder T. J. Watson. Statistics say that 44 percent of salespeople give up after the first no, 22 percent more give up after the second no, 14 percent more give up after the third no, and 12 percent more give up after the fourth no. Do the math, and you will realize that 92 percent of salespeople give up by the fourth attempt. On the other hand, a study suggests that 60 percent of customers say no four times before they finally say yes the fifth time.

There are no easy sales. Customers will always start by saying no to whatever you sell to protect themselves from any new things they are unaware of. It is just part of human nature to say no to the unknowns.

However, the word no does not mean no. It means, "I didn't understand you," or, "Try a different approach," or, "I am busy now. Discuss it with me later," and so on. Unfortunately, average salespeople stop after the first attempt, thinking that the customer did not agree to the proposition. This is a big problem.

Average RMs take the rejection personally and never attempt to reopen the discussion with the customer. If you don't like being rejected, maybe you are in the wrong position. If you are not willing to change your mindset, change your career. Staying in sales without being persistent is a mistake.

FOLLOW UP WITH "WHY?"

Salespeople should be smart and must understand why the customer is saying no. The answer will help you identify the gaps, so you can do your best to bridge them in order to close the deal. You should not press on without understanding the reasons for rejection. Most of those reasons don't make sense. Let's look at a few:

- The current solution is better than what you are suggesting.
- The management did not accept your offer.
- We don't have time for this now.
- The current system is working fine. We don't want to disturb anything.
- I am paying less than what the proposed solution would cost me.

None of these rejections are valid from the sales standpoint. There is no place to sell if you believe these reasons to be true. Try to dig deeper and understand *why* the customer is not ready to discuss the solution you think will add immense value to them.

Pressing on without changing your sales approach will not help much either. When you hear no, change the sales story, address the most important things to them, and elaborate extensively on how you can help. Dive deep into the gap analysis and try to find all the gaps you can fill—show the real value of your solution.

The customer may not be interested in your solution because they didn't understand you properly. Therefore, you must speak to them from their own perspective. Focus on the areas that they value the most. Try a totally different approach by speaking to somebody else in the organization. Maybe the person you are speaking to is not interested in delivering value to the organization.

LISTEN TO UNSPOKEN REJECTION

"The most important thing in communication is hearing what isn't said," said Peter Drucker. Tune into what the customer isn't saying.

Empathetic salespeople are great at connecting with the customers, and they try to understand what the customers are thinking or feeling, then try to pull the rejection up to the surface to deal with it.

Here is a scenario of a customer who has recently bought a new CRM system, but it is not up to her expectations. She wants an alternative but is reluctant because she doesn't want to make the mistake of buying a wrong solution again. An empathetic salesperson would tune into the customer's feelings and say something like this: "I understand that you have just bought a new CRM and it is not up to your expectations. If I were you, I would certainly be asking myself about the capabilities of the new vendor and whether their product will solve all the issues we currently have. The second concern I would have is whether the change is really worth it. Valid concerns. Am I reading this correctly?"

Now the conversation has shifted from unspoken rejection to a deep dive into the real issues that are preventing the change. The customer will be open to talking more and saying what she actually feels. Bringing unspoken objections to the surface is a great strategy to make the customer listen to you.

CREATING A SENSE OF URGENCY

Creating a sense of urgency is what top performers do to encourage the customer to change from saying no to saying yes. Asking the customer to change something that is not a priority for them leads to resistance because you are proposing to disrupt the status quo, and the solution offered will require some sort of change on their part.

On a scale of 1 to 10, with 1 being the lowest and 10 being the highest, how do you rate the customer's pain? The closer it is to 10, the easier it is to convince the customer to change. Find the pressing issues, focus on them, and get the customer to agree that there is a problem.

We base our decisions on social proof and tend to do what others do. One of the best methods for creating a sense of urgency is sharing case studies of other customers. The incident could be about a customer who benefited from the solution in terms of money, productivity, or enhancement. Or it could be about an unpleasant scenario where a bad thing happened to another customer because they delayed implementing the solution you offer. For example, say you are trying to get a customer to move from an in-house data center to a cloud environment. It will be a big task for the customer to implement this change. However, if you create a sense of urgency by sharing an incident about a customer who lost the entire data center because of a fire, resulting in a loss of vital data and expensive hardware, it will make them think seriously about it and urge them to change the status quo as soon as possible. Showing the customer the cost/benefit analysis will create an enormous sense of urgency, especially when the benefit is huge or the gap is big.

The bigger the gap, the easier it is to win the deal. A couple of years ago, I took my son Khalid to the hospital, as he was not feeling well. He was seven years old at the time. It was hard for him to describe the pain. However, the hospital had created a system to measure the pain and prioritize those in severe pain. They handed a piece of paper to my son—a happy face with a 0 on the left side and a sad face with a 10 underneath it on the right side—and asked him to evaluate his pain. Khalid chose 9 on the scale, and we were immediately taken to the doctor on a priority basis.

I want you to be the doctor and focus on the customers who are in great pain and closer to a 10. Selling to the ones who are in severe pain is easier than selling to those in mild pain. Be strategic about whom to go after first. The ones who are closer to 1 on the pain scale are not your priority at the moment. Ask them to wait till after you go and treat those in severe pain.

YOU DON'T WANT LIFE INSURANCE, DO YOU?

In his book, *Go for No!* Richard Fenton has shared an interesting story about a life insurance company's executive who hired a consultant to fix his sales team. After studying all the available information, the consultant was ready to present the findings. They met with the executive and told him that his sales team was not making enough calls and that this was the root cause of all the problems. With utter surprise, the executive said, "I did not pay you to give me this simple answer."

The consultant replied, "It is true, and I will prove it to you."

A salesperson was averaging two sales per month before hiring the consultant. The consultant's plan was to devise a negative message but ask every salesperson to make sixty sales calls a day. The consultant asked the salespeople to use the following negative message with every customer they encountered: "You don't want life insurance, do you?" Fifty-eight out of sixty customers said, "You are right. We don't want life insurance." But there were two customers who said, "As a matter of fact, I am looking for life insurance. Tell me more about it."

After having averaged two sales a month, every salesperson closed two deals per day. Not bad!

This story shows that you should never give up, despite the obstacles that come your way. You must focus on your goal, even when you don't know how you will succeed. Think about only one outcome—success. Failure should never be an option. Try multiple times and multiple ways until it happens. Be courageous and unafraid of rejection. Persist and persevere.

Chapter 10

MINDSET #5 – RELATIONSHIPS

Building meaningful relationships within an account is what differentiates the ultra-high performers from the average ones. Top producers know the importance of relationships. They have deep relationships with C-level executives and other important stakeholders. However, building meaningful relationships with everyone in the account is not easy. The investment you make in building relationships with the decision-makers and influencers in advance will pay off when the right time comes.

On the other hand, underperformers attempt to acquaint themselves with the decision-makers when they are stuck in a deal. To put it simply, the underperformers don't come close to the word *relationship*, let alone *meaningful*. They merely have a business connection with their accounts, as opposed to a relationship. They are anchored to one person, and if, for any reason, this person decides not to pursue an opportunity, they are sunk. And, yes, this will always be the case. They start the chase and look for the CEO's and CIO's LinkedIn profiles, and before they know it, the deal goes somewhere else.

Meaningful relationships, without a doubt, lead to winning the customer's business. Many customers buy products they don't even need. They buy because the salesperson they like and have a relationship with recommended the product. Once, I asked a salesperson who was short on his target by $20,000, "How did you manage to achieve the target in the last week of the month?" He said, "I asked the customer to buy the product even though they didn't have an immediate requirement for it."

In many instances, salespeople close deals despite their prices being higher than the competition's for the same product. Why would a customer pay a higher price for a product from a salesperson they know versus a lower price for the same product from a salesperson they don't know? The customer pays more because their relationship manager understands them better than the competition does. The relationship manager is always on their side and within reach whenever the client wants.

Building meaningful relationships doesn't happen overnight. Here are a few ideas for building strong relationships within the account:

1- Know the client personally. Here are a few things you should try to know about your customer:

   a. Where they come from, their background in terms of career, and how long they have been working for their company.

   b. Their birthday. Wishing them a happy birthday means a lot to them.

   c. Information about their family; for example, how many kids they have and what their names are. So when you meet them, ask about their kids by name.

d. Their interests. For example, ask about the team they cheer for, so you can send them a message when their favorite team wins. Or talk about a healthy lifestyle if they are into that.

2- Call the client regularly, not necessarily to sell them something. Just call and ask about their health, work, and kids.

3- Be closer to them and go out for lunch with them.

4- Engage in physical activities with them, such as walking, running, or playing tennis.

5- Connect with them on social media, i.e., Facebook, Instagram, LinkedIn, Twitter, and other social media platforms. You can learn a lot about them, their interests, places they visit, countries they travel to, sports they follow, music they listen to, and much more.

Be genuinely interested in them as people before being interested in their business. Get closer to them. Invest your time in building strong bonds that would be hard for the competition to break. Establish trusting, open, and friendly relationships that are built on creating value for them and proving that you are someone worth doing business with.

AVOID RELATIONSHIP GAPS

Sometimes, relationship gaps are created by the relationship managers themselves. In many instances, they don't pick up the customers' call, they don't address the customers' problems when they arise, or they are not there when their customers need them. To make matters worse, they sell unsuitable solutions that stifle the relationship with their customers.

Acts of neglect will undoubtedly create a huge relationship gap that is very hard to bridge. When the time comes, these salespeople try to sell a product to the same person whose call was not answered.

I remember a client called me and complained about a salesperson who didn't answer the phone when she called. I was surprised because the client worked for a decent company, and this salesperson could have sold several solutions to this client. I called the salesperson to validate what the client said. When I asked him if he really didn't pick up when she called, he said, "Maybe she called after working hours. I usually keep my phone in my car after working hours." What a shocking reply from a salesperson who wants to win his customers' business but treats his most important client this way. Ouch!

SOLVING A CUSTOMER PROBLEM

Sometimes, the first meeting with the customer goes wrong and they complain about the negative experiences they have had with your company. This may not have been your fault, and now you have to deal with the mess someone else created before you. This is a blessing in disguise. You should be happy that the customer is complaining about a particular issue, because it gives you an opportunity to show that you care and will go all the way to solve their problems. Problems that are raised by customers are actually opportunities to strengthen your relationship with them.

Solve your clients' issues, and you will build a long and trusting relationship with them. Turn your back on these problems, and your chances of building a long-lasting relationship with your dream clients will vanish.

STAKEHOLDER MAPPING—BASIC

A relationship with the account doesn't mean that you know only one person in the company. It means you know all the stakeholders and, most importantly, the decision-makers. I agree, this may not happen overnight, but this should be your ultimate objective. One of the main issues with average salespeople is that they bang their heads against one person in the company. It is an obvious concern, because this person may not be interested in bringing value to the company they work for, or they could be busy and not paying attention to you. They may even be planning to leave the company very soon.

Job Blount, in his book *Sales EQ*, says that there are five stakeholders you meet in most deals: buyers, amplifiers, seekers, influencers, and coaches—BASIC. High performers in sales understand the importance of mapping stakeholders early in the deal; they get to know all the stakeholders and leave nothing to chance.

Buyers

There are two types of *buyers*: buyers who can say yes to the commitment, authorize the deal, and sign the contract, and buyers who can only fund the project and write the check. For example, the CIO can finalize the deal and says yes to the solution, but nothing will happen unless the CFO agrees to fund the project.

Early engagement of the stakeholders who will impact your deal is necessary to win the deal. Don't be intimidated by the titles; you are worthy of meeting the C-suite executives. Nothing much will happen at the point of contact level; therefore, leveling up to the decision-makers early in the deal is essential for gaining a competitive advantage.

Amplifiers

Amplifiers are stakeholders who see a problem or a gap your product can bridge. They are advocates for change and amplify the message of change. High performers are masters at leveraging the relationship with amplifiers to pass the message to the decision-makers for an immediate need for change.

Seekers

Seekers are stakeholders who usually look for information, download e-books, and attend webinars. They have little or no buying authority or influence. Many deals are stalled and never move to the next stage because average salespeople are stuck with seekers and never level up to the other key stakeholders.

Influencers

Influencers are stakeholders who play an active role in the deal. High performers understand the importance of building relationships with influencers to bend the winning probability in their favor. Influencers are usually either your advocates or naysayers. Pay attention—most of the time, your deals are stalled because of influencers.

Coaches

Coaches are stakeholders who are willing to help you and provide insider information. Building a strong relationship with coaches is important, as they will be your advocate inside the organization. They can advise if there are any upcoming problems or opportunities.

High performers in sales understand the importance of building meaningful relationships with all the stakeholders within an account. They map the stakeholders correctly at every stage of the pipeline. I see many deals stall because the salesperson is comfortable dealing with one stakeholder and never puts in the effort to look beyond that person. Talking to one person in the organization helps in a few cases, but in many instances, it doesn't. Sometimes, the deal gets lost just because of the disengagement of your point of contact in the organization.

I often hear from salespeople that they were in discussion with the IT manager and the deal was hot and would close in one month, only to learn after a few months that the customer had signed with another vendor. He learned later that the admin in charge had decided to sign with another vendor without the alignment of the IT team. Think for a moment; if the salesperson engaged with all the stakeholders in the company who are likely to decide early in the discussion, he would have had more insight about the deal and the competition. Ask the person you usually deal with: When is the right time to engage the other stakeholders in the discussion, CEO, CIO, CFO, IT, admin, HR, etc.?

Building relationships with all the stakeholders in any organization will take time. Don't wait till you get closer to closing a deal—start from the first day of engagement. Trying to level up to the CEO or another person in the organization in the middle of the deal may not be in your favor, and it could upset your point of contact.

PEOPLE BUY FROM PEOPLE THEY LIKE

The first impression is about likability, and likability is the gateway to building relationships with customers. When the customer likes you, they will be open to hearing from you and answering all of your questions. Keep one thing in mind: Customers don't buy from someone they don't like. There are many aspects of likability that are beyond your control, like your gender, race, and language. On the other hand, many are under your direct control.

KEYS TO BEING MORE LIKABLE

1- Smile: A pleasant and sincere smile is the best way to make the first impression. People are usually attracted to those who smile.

2- Voice: Your tone should be natural and free from any made-up dialects. Just be yourself and use a normal tone of voice.

3- Be polite: It is very important to be polite and avoid any actions that would come off as rude in front of the customer.

4- Dress: People will judge you by what you wear, what you drive, and how you smell. People like to do business with other people who have an attractive appearance.

5- Grooming: Ensure that you smell nice and that your hair, facial hair, and nails are clean. Cover up your tattoos if you have them, as they are considered inappropriate in some countries.

6- Attention: It is easy to be distracted by your phone or laptop when connecting with the customer over the phone or at their office. Ensure that you are completely focused and present with the customer. You would feel angry if the person you were talking to was busy with his/her smartphone rather than with you. Customers feel the same way. Failure to listen damages connections and destroys relationships. The number one complaint clients make is that salespeople don't listen. When they are given a chance to talk, they block their ears and keep pitching, and even when they are not talking, they are thinking about what to say next. If salespeople would start paying attention to what the customer is saying, they would be able to identify the customer's problems easily and start working on the solution. Despite all the training that salespeople take on listening, it is still the weakest link in human interaction. It is challenging to do the following:

- Stay away from the distractions around you.
- Wait for your turn to talk without interrupting.
- Avoid looking down at your phone screen.
- Turn off your thoughts and pay attention to the customer.
- Remain interested when you find other people boring.

Most people believe they have control when they talk. It is actually the other way around. You control the conversation when you listen and ask, as you are directing the conversation the way you want.

Chapter 11

MINDSET #6 – GROWTH

There are many aspects of our lives that we should intentionally work on and improve, such as mental, physical, social, and spiritual. All these attributes impact how we live and, particularly, how we perform in sales, especially the mental and physical aspects. Let's look at them in turn.

MENTAL

Research conducted by Tom Corley, author of *Change Your Habits, Change Your Life*, found that 88 percent of wealthy people dedicate thirty minutes for self-development daily, compared to 2 percent of the non-wealthy. Tony Robbins, a well-known life coach and motivational speaker, shared a story of how he gained knowledge by reading seven hundred books in seven years. Many other super-successful people in business attribute their success to building a huge knowledge base, and dedicate five to ten hours a week for learning and growing.

Mike Weinberg, author of *Sales Truth*, says that if you are not learning, you are dying. Think for a moment and answer this question:

How many books have you read on sales? If you are like most average salespeople, you would probably say zero. If your answer is few to none, how do you expect to learn and grow?

You are lucky if you are successful without investing in yourself, but it usually doesn't happen that way. People who don't learn are at the mercy of the customers and count on others to give them business.

Learning and growing is in quadrant two, the Schedule quadrant, which is for important but not urgent tasks. If you don't plan for it, don't expect for it to happen on its own. An average CEO reads about fifty-two books a year, which is one book a week. I'm not sure if you are busier than a CEO; however, considering your tight schedule and your background with minimal reading, I presume a book a week would be difficult to achieve, at least in the beginning. You can start with a book a month, and then you can build it up to a book every two weeks. Think about it. By the end of the year, you will finish twenty-four books, and in two years, you will have read almost fifty books. Just imagine yourself today with your limited knowledge, compared to yourself after reading fifty books in two years. Which version of yourself do you think will know more, be smarter, and have better business acumen?

Commuting from home to work and vice versa consumes a massive amount of time. To make the commute time productive, listening to audiobooks in your car is a great habit. You will be surprised by the amount of knowledge you can gain only by listening to audiobooks. Let's do a quick math together. If you take thirty minutes to go to work and another thirty minutes to reach home, that adds up to five hours of commute time a week. Five hours is the approximate amount of time you need to listen to and finish one audiobook. This means you can finish one book a week only by listening, which translates to fifty audiobooks in a year.

I have turned my car into a moving library. I have listened to 160 audiobooks in five years covering many topics, especially sales. This is an easy way to get productive in your car, as opposed to listening to radio channels or music. I love it when I get stuck in traffic, because I know the more time I spend in the car, the more knowledge I'll gain. It also removes all the stress around traffic and honking at one another. You will not only be calm and relaxed, but also you will enjoy listening to the author reading his book to you. It doesn't get better than that.

Enhancing Business Acumen

Enhancing business acumen is extremely important to set yourself up for success and strike meaningful and relevant conversations with your dream clients. It's a way of demonstrating your expertise as a trusted adviser in the industry.

Continuous improvement leads to sustainable success in sales. Ultra-high performers make time to remain relevant within the industry. They set aside time daily to enhance their business acumen around sales and other topics related to their industry. If you work in the telecom industry, for instance, you could enhance your knowledge on things like artificial intelligence, machine learning, robotics, 5G, cybersecurity, blockchain, IoT, multi-cloud, and other trending technologies. It is extremely essential to learn about every product you sell. Be the expert in your domain and see your sales career skyrocket.

Rewiring Your Brain

According to neuroscientists, reading not only fills your brain with information, but it also rewires how your brain works in general.

Reading plays a crucial part in keeping our brain fit and healthy. It increases cognitive function, enhances long- and short-term memory, and stimulates creative problem-solving. Reading is something worth factoring into your daily routine, just like brushing your teeth or going to the gym. Every page you flip keeps your brain young. It provides mental exercise, which is critical to prevent memory decline. Your brain is a learning machine—it has to keep learning to optimize its performance and improve its thinking ability.

Here are some resources you can use for learning and growing:

- Udemy: A great self-learning portal at an affordable price. You can learn about any subject you are interested in, for example, AI, blockchain, or Excel.
- Audible: This is one of the best audiobook platforms you can use while driving or walking.
- E-books: Many platforms are available for reading e-books, including Amazon Kindle, Google Playbook, Kobo, and many more.

PHYSICAL

I am not going to start talking about how exercise will benefit your health. Many have covered this topic widely, and you are well aware of the value of physical activity to your overall health. However, what many don't know is how exercise can transform your brain. Physical and mental wellness are intertwined; they are ideal for optimizing brain function and reducing stress. Based on experience, I address how physical activity will affect your sales profession in a positive way.

In her research, Wendy Suzuki found that exercise is the most transformative thing you can do for your brain. Exercise enhances your mood right after the workout, improves your focus and attention, and speeds up your reaction time, which leads to better decision-making in business. She also found that exercise creates new brain cells that can improve long-term memory and enhances overall brain function.

Exercise makes you look and feel good. Working out, preferably in the morning, will ensure that you are ready to work with full energy. It is also a way to defuse your stress and anger and approach work with a positive mindset. Dedicating one hour, four times a week, to some sort of physical activity will have a great impact on your sales profession. It could be running, cycling, swimming, aerobic training, HIIT, weightlifting, power walking, or any other physical activity.

To maintain a healthy lifestyle and boost your sales performance, physical activity is not enough. It has to be combined with a balanced and healthy diet. High-energy foods are essential to keep you charged and ready for the challenges of sales. Taking care of your body is also an important part of the process. Sleeping well is key if you desire to take your sales career to the next level. You can't expect to be excited to get to work if you go to bed late and report to work exhausted and fatigued. Regenerating energy through good sleep is a priority if you want to be among the top sales professionals. Six to eight hours of sleep are necessary for renewed energy.

Chapter 12
MINDSET REFLECTION

Success in sales largely depends on mindset. Just as in life, in sales, mindset determines the outcome of your performance. It creates the foundation for mastery and the backbone of any pursuit of excellence. Are you emotionally intelligent enough to recognize when negativity or self-doubt creeps into your mind? Colleen Stanley, the author of *Emotional Intelligence for Sales Leadership*, suggests, "That which you are not aware of, you cannot change. That which you are not aware of, you are bound to repeat." Emotionally intelligent salespeople recognize themselves in the middle of negative self-talk or being reactive, and immediately change.

Tip: A rule of thumb for many; referred to as the *5-minute rule*, allows you to deal with a negative outcome and negative emotion. Give yourself 5 minutes to let the negative feeling drain out of you, and then get back to work.

The muscle of self-awareness needs to be developed and strengthened over time. Taking downtime every day in the morning to review what went well the day before and what to avoid in the future is a powerful habit and an effective way to manage one's mindset. It is necessary to remind yourself every day—every single day—of the power of discipline, proactivity, positivity, persistence, relationship, and growth, until these traits are part of your character. Different research suggests that it takes anywhere from sixteen to forty days to attain a particular trait by repeating and reminding yourself. Affirmations play a vital role here; don't be afraid to fake it till you make it.

We are used to doing things a certain way and stop paying attention to how we could improve. It's easy to let mistakes slide. When you want to maximize your potential and achieve an elite level of performance, you need a new approach. Like Einstein put it, "Insanity is doing the same thing over and over again and expecting different results."

Mastering each mindset element unlocks a higher level of performance. What we need is a way to remain conscious of our perspective over time to develop and improve. The solution is to establish a system for reflection and review. Great athletes reflect and review their performance every day. For example, the greatest marathon runner of all time, Eliud Kipchoge, still takes notes after every practice and searches for areas of development.

In his book *Atomic Habits*, James Clear talks about the compounding effect of 1 percent improvement every day. Take any area of your life, review it, and see how it improves. A minor enhancement every day leads to great results by the end of the year.

Being aware of your state of mind is the first step toward change. Take downtime, reflect on your mindset every day, and ask yourself the following questions:

- Am I a disciplined person? Do I stick to my plan and do what I say I will do? If the answer is yes, can I share an example that shows my discipline? If the answer is no, what will I do about it?

- Am I a proactive person? Do I make things happen? If the answer is yes, can I share an example that shows my proactivity? If the answer is no, what will I do about it?

- Am I a positive person? Do I look at the positive side even in tough times? If the answer is yes, can I share an example that shows my positivity? If the answer is no, what will I do about it?

- Am I a persistent person? Do I press ahead without giving up? If the answer is yes, can I share an example that shows my persistence? If the answer is no, what will I do about it?

- Am I good at building meaningful relationships? Do I have the EQ to build meaningful relationships? If the answer is yes, can I share an example that shows my EQ with people? If the answer is no, what will I do about it?

- Am I learning and growing? Do I learn and grow in my domain? Do I dedicate time to improve my business acumen? If the answer is yes, can I share an example that shows my willingness to learn and grow? If the answer is no, what will I do about it?

HOW HEALTHY IS YOUR MINDSET?

Based on the above self-evaluation questions, how do you rate your mindset on a scale of 1 to 5? Sometimes, the evaluation will be subjective. Try your best with real examples.

Mindset evaluation matrix:

Scale	Current state	Ideal state	Gap
Discipline	4	5	1
Proactivity	3	5	2
Positivity	2.5	5	2.5
Persistence	3	5	2
Relationships	4	5	1
Growth	2	5	3
Total	**18.5**	**30**	**62%**

How healthy is your mindset? The example in the table shows that this person's mindset health is at 62 percent (18.5, your current score divided by 30, the ideal score). Evaluate your mindset and figure out the percentage you are at and where you want to be. What is your action plan to improve the score of every element of your mindset, and by when? Write it down and decide on the next mindset evaluation date. Ideally, taking downtime to reflect every day on your mindset is the best model; however, a self-evaluation activity like this should be carried out every month, making sure you track your progress and plan to reach your goals.

CRACKING THE SALES CODE

THE SECRET FORMULA TO UNLOCK YOUR SALES POTENTIAL IN BUSINESS SALES

Part III
SKILLSET

Chapter 13

SALES COMBAT ZONE

The Sales Code can't be cracked unless we address the skillset element of the MST formula. This is where the rubber meets the road. Let's unfold two of the most lethal sales weapons: (1) the sales story and (2) the sales pipeline. Mastering the skillset will enable you to reach an elite level of performance in your domain.

The performance gap between the top producers and the underperformers becomes visible when we address the sales story and sales pipeline management. The top achievers understand the importance of their skillset and do whatever it takes to get it right. On the other hand, average performers depend primarily on luck and pray that they will stumble upon something good one day.

PREPARED FOR THE BATTLE

There are many aspects of the sales marketplace that resemble a battlefield. In wars, the most qualified soldiers are enlisted, undergo rigorous training programs, and prepare from a mindset and a skillset standpoint to be ready for the battle. Have you ever seen a soldier going to the combat zone without knowing how to fire a weapon, let alone having one? If you have, you know that poor soldier would not have made it out of the battleground, right? Similarly, in sales, sending salespeople to market without the right sales weapon is an act of suicide. What will happen to them? Exactly! So what is the point of sending them, anyway? Apart from everything else, it's an utter waste of opportunity. Without a proper sales weapon, it is impossible to win the client's business. RMs should avoid going to market if they are not prepared from the skillset perspective. If they don't have the skillset, there is a high probability every business opportunity will go down the drain.

When a window of opportunity cracks open with a customer, we should leverage it and never miss a chance. Opportunity is just as important as your ability to capitalize on it. How do we achieve that and ensure we don't blow our chances? The RM should be able to deliver a compelling sales story that increases the likelihood of creating an opportunity, artfully moving the deals through multiple stages in the pipeline, and ultimately closing the deal.

There is a 20 percent chance of creating an opportunity during the first encounter with any client. It is entirely up to the RM to pull it down to 0 percent or build it up to 40, 80, and, ultimately, 100 percent.

What are the deciding factors? You got that right: the skillset. If the RM is mediocre at his sales story, he will plunge every opportunity to 0 percent. On the other hand, if he masters the sales story, the win probability for every deal rises toward closure, most of the time. The relationship manager may not be able to close every deal. Still, if the win probability was elevated to 40 or 80 percent, it was at least a good try, rather than failing miserably at every attempt. Be fair to yourself, and don't be among those who let every opportunity slip through their fingers just because they don't have a convincing sales story or know how to manage the sales pipeline. Most importantly, please do not fall into the trap of blame, thinking of why it was not your fault the deal didn't close.

The main challenge I have noticed with some relationship managers is that everyone has their own sales story. While some of them have a good sales story, some have mediocre ones, some have bad ones, and some don't have one at all. As a result, they struggle, and after a few unstructured attempts, they lose interest and ultimately give up—unfortunately, a typical problem faced by average salespeople. Thankfully, we are here to address these concerns. By the end of the book, you will be able to create a compelling sales story for every product you sell. Nobody should suffer as we will learn together how to take a clear message to market that guarantees the creation of many more qualified opportunities than you can handle. Once the opportunity is created, we will learn how to advance it through multiple stages in the sales pipeline by asking for commitments from the customer that propel the deal forward.

My main objective is to transform your go-to-market strategy and show you the way to success. In this section of the book, we will reveal a sales weapon with which you ideally will be able to create high-value opportunities, seamlessly move them through the pipeline, and eventually close the deals all by yourself. Ready when you are!

Chapter 14

THE SALES STORY

Is it the *sales story* or the *sales pitch*? I do not personally fancy the term *sales pitch*, as many make their first mistake here. I would rather call it a *sales story* because stories are more fun to tell and are more interesting to hear. I give a ton of credit to author and motivational speaker Mike Weinberg, who introduced the sales story concept in his book *New Sales Simplified*. It is a great book, and I recommend that you pick it up.

A story has five essential elements: character, setting, plot, conflict, and resolution. These elements are told in sequence. If you try to tell a story starting from the resolution or conflict, then immediately start talking about the character, the listener will be confused, there will be no flow to the tale, and the story will be dull. The sales story is similar. There are vital elements, and they have to be told in a sequence to avoid confusing yourself and confounding the customer.

Average salespeople don't have a story to tell, and every time they meet a customer, they come up with a different, fragile version. They try to experiment with different ideas without assessing the practicality behind what may work. As a result, they deliver a chaotic pitch, and the probability of creating an opportunity dwindles.

PUTTING THE CART IN FRONT OF THE HORSE

As a sales consultant, you need to understand the customer first, then propose a solution. It doesn't work the other way around. You cannot offer a solution and then try to understand the customer's issues. It is like putting the cart in front of the horse. Think about it—if you are offering a solution before understanding the customer first, ask yourself: "Solution to what?" if you still don't know what the issue is.

For the story to be interesting, it has to be about the customer. Your story will be boring if it is about you or your product. Losing the customer's attention happens in just a few seconds if they feel the discussion is not about them, especially if it is a telephonic conversation. The customer is always interested in listening to what is relevant to them. They want to discuss their problems and the impact of these problems on their business. Top producers share a well-crafted sales story that shows the existing problems or the future opportunities the client may not know about and how they can work together to address them. This is where your role as a sales professional becomes critical.

On many occasions, the customer will tell you that they don't have time and will push you to deliver your sales story in less than five minutes. You get nervous and try to squeeze out everything you know about the product in the given time. As a result, you deliver a less-than-adequate product pitch that is neither related nor tailored to that particular customer's business, which is precisely why average salespeople have an empty pipeline. If you find yourself in this situation, tell the customer that you want to understand the nature of their business and figure out if your solution is a perfect fit for them. Then you will call them tomorrow to learn more about them and their business. The customer needs to realize that you are there to offer them a tailored solution rather than a pitch you've memorized and used way too often for nothing but personal benefit.

Mediocre salespeople talk about the power of the *elevator pitch*. What can you sell from the first floor to the tenth floor? It is barely five seconds. Nothing can be sold in five seconds or five minutes! If you are in a retail store and there is a long line in front of you, by all means, use the elevator pitch. However, the same concept does not work in business sales.

The sales story is the most essential and critical tool in sales. Get it right, and success is inevitable. Let's discuss the elements of the sales story and how to craft your own from the ground up for every product or solution in your portfolio.

Chapter 15

SALES STORY STRUCTURE

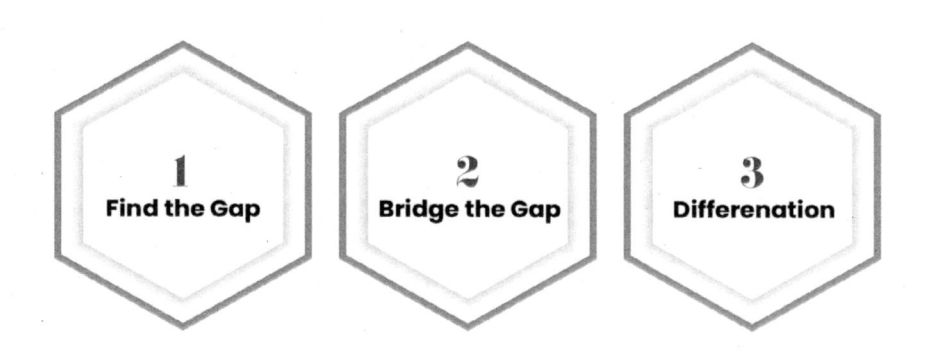

1	2	3
Find the Gap	**Bridge the Gap**	**Differenation**

The sales story is divided into three broad parts. The first part is *Find the Gap*, the second part is *Bridge the Gap*, and the final piece is *Differentiation*. The Find the Gap part of the sales story is the most important. Eighty percent of your time should be spent finding the gap and convincing the customer to agree that there is an issue that needs to be addressed. It doesn't have to be literal, as this gap could also be an opportunity that needs to be capitalized on. The Bridge the Gap or Differentiation stage should not precede the Find the Gap stage whatsoever unless the customer knows the problem and is looking for a solution.

Here are the building blocks of every stage of the sales story framework. (We will be discussing each element in detail in the following pages.)

P #1: Find the Gap:
- Setting expectations
- Probing
- Agreement
- Power statement
- Discovery
- Creating a sense of urgency
- Engaging the stakeholders
- Summarizing the gap

P #2: Bridge the Gap:
- Solution
- Demo of the product
- Price

P #3: Differentiation:
- How your solution is superior to all other offers in the market

SALES STORY P #1: FIND THE GAP

Understand this in simple terms: there is no sale if there is no problem. Period, end of story. A sales discussion is always centered on the customer's concerns and issues. It is never about your product or solution.

An absolute empty pipeline will be the outcome if you try to do it the other way around. It could even be the most superior product or service out there, but that's not what I want you to focus on, at least not now, no matter how much you want to. Remember, it all starts with a problem.

The first few seconds of the discussion with the customer are critical. You either lose them or hold their attention. If, for any reason, they feel the discussion is not about them and has nothing to do with their business, they will not be interested in carrying on. To avoid this risk, your sales story should start with a deep discovery session to identify all the gaps that may impact the client's business. Sometimes, the gaps are apparent to you, but not to the customer. Informing the customer about the problems and the impact they have or will have on their business becomes your first and only mission.

Think about it. If the gaps were visible to the customer, wouldn't they have addressed them before you even approached them? Absolutely. That is why most of the time, the customer is unaware of the existence of such gaps and the impact of those gaps on their business.

It is advised that you do your homework before approaching the customer; we call this *pre-call planning*. Analyze the customer's current state, particularly about his business, and all potential problems the customer could have ahead of time. You can relate to their competition or the industry in general. Most customers face generic problems in a particular sector, and this is your first point of reference.

Once the gaps have been identified, their impact has been made evident to the customer, and the customer has agreed that there is a problem. Pat yourself on the back for doing a brilliant job. The customer is now intrigued to know more about the issue and the magnitude of its impact. More often than not, if the problem is big enough, the customer will chase you to help bridge the gap, and for the first time, you no longer need to continue chasing.

Notice how we have not even started to talk about our product, or how it is better than the competition's. We only took an interest in the customer's business and wanted to examine the current state of the customer to identify the problem and its impact on their business. That's it.

Now let's unfold the Find the Gap stage of the sales story framework, one step at a time.

1. Setting expectations
2. Probing
3. Agreement
4. Power statement
5. Discovery
6. Creating a sense of urgency
7. Engaging the stakeholders
8. Summarizing the gap

SETTING EXPECTATIONS

The first task in the Find the Gap stage is to set the right expectations. Managing expectations sounds easy until emotion gets in the way. Average salespeople pull the customer toward their product without setting any expectations. Being clear on your goal for this call and the amount of time required to understand the customer's current situation is crucial.

Let's look at two scenarios. Read the examples below and evaluate each salesperson's approach:

Salesperson 1: Hi Ameer, I know you are busy. I'd like to have five minutes of your time to go over our cloud solution. (Then they jump straight to the product.)

What is wrong with this approach? Everything. Let's analyze.

First, the salesperson assumes that the customer is busy and won't get the time he or she wants. In fact, this is why average salespeople are in trouble: assumption on top of another assumption. They start to tell themselves stories and believe them, and end up deciding on behalf of the customer. Ask the customer and give them a chance to respond. Do not assume. Just because your last customer said he was busy does not mean the next one is too. Every client is a new opportunity and could be completely opposite from your previous one.

The second problem here is that the salesperson said he or she needed five minutes of the client's time, which is not true; nothing can be sold in five minutes. Be clear on how much time you need. If they say they are busy, schedule another meeting with them sometime later. Ask them what time is their preferred time to be contacted. If they are unsure, pitch them a time and day and confirm it with them.

Third, the salesperson said that he wanted to talk about his cloud solution and jumped straight to the product discussion. Pitching the product at this point in time is clearly not setting the stage for a consultative sales meeting and is undoubtedly not a smart move. It is still about you and your product, which is the least of the customer's concerns at this stage.

On the other hand, assertive sales professionals set clear expectations, state precisely what they need, and always pay attention to the customer first rather than their product. Check this approach out:

Salesperson: Hi Ameer, I would like to talk about a solution that I believe will add value to your company. In order to explore that with you, I will be asking a few questions to check if our solution is the right fit for your company. To understand and evaluate the situation with you, I will need about twenty minutes to discuss the challenges and goals. Will that work for you?

Let us discuss why the second scenario is more effective and assertive. The salesperson provided three critical messages to the customer about what he or she would do:

1- Provide value to the client
2- Explore and find a perfect fit between the product and the client's business issues
3- Do these things in a set amount of time

The first message the salesperson sends out indicates that he or she has value to offer to the client's business and wants to explore that further. If there is no value to offer here, the salesperson will guide them to someone else.

The second message the salesperson is trying to communicate is that he or she is not going to sell anything but rather is interested in figuring out with the customer if the product or solution is a perfect fit for their business or not. The salesperson puts the customer's amygdala (part of the brain that drives the fight-or-flight response) at ease by telling them, in essence, "I will walk away if there is not a perfect fit between my solution and your company's current or future state."

The third message is setting clear expectations in terms of how much time you need to explore the situation with them. If the customer is in the middle of something critical, they are not going to pay attention. Moreover, if they have a meeting with their CEO in the next thirty minutes, they will not give you the undivided attention you want. If the customer says they are busy, it is a perfect moment to schedule an appointment for an hour on a date and time when they are available.

Notice the difference between the two scenarios. Observe how the salesperson in the second scenario sets clear expectations in terms of the need to have a dialogue with the customer and the amount of time needed to go through the discovery phase to figure out if the solution is the right fit for the client's company.

Once the expectations are established and the customer is open to discussion, next comes probing.

PROBING

The second step in Find the Gap stage is *probing*. We realized how important it is to understand the customer's problems first and then propose a solution. It does not work the other way around. Unfortunately, average RMs jump to the pitch without understanding the customer's *situation*. Sometimes, you just need to walk away because there is no problem to address nor opportunity for you to capture. Perhaps the customer will need your solution in the future, but not now. So just walk away. Do not sell to someone who does not need what you have to offer. More importantly, do not waste your time in doing so. Be wise enough to value your time by filtering and speaking to potential customers.

The probing stage is vital in determining whether to carry on with the sales story or stop. The first few questions should be designed to enable you to identify the potential customers to target. Picture this:

you make arrangements to meet with an important client to talk about a cloud solution. You discuss the solution in detail, only to find out in the middle of the discussion that the customer is already on the cloud or does not have any servers at all. Ouch, how embarrassing is that?

Another mistake that many relationship managers fall for is asking too many questions in the probing stage. Probing questions should be designed in a way that it doesn't sound like an interrogation. The customer will probably be irritated if you ask too many questions, especially at the beginning of the session. The probing questions should be limited to two or three open-ended questions. Every question you ask has to capture valuable information in deciding whether to carry on with the discussion or just stop. Also, try to avoid budget-related questions early on that may give your client the impression that you are just another salesperson interested in emptying their pocket. An individual defines himself with the questions he asks, so be careful what your questions say about you.

Going back to the cloud example, imagine if you ask these probing questions to the customer at the beginning of the discussion:

- Where are the servers hosted?
- How many people are managing these servers?
- How much do you pay them?
- How many servers do you have?
- What are these servers for?
- Have you experienced business continuity issues with these servers?
- Is scalability important to you?

How would you feel if your relationship manager fired these unprepared questions at you? It would feel like an interrogation, partly because the customer may not even know who you are and what you are up to.

What should I do if I have a lot of questions? The answer is simple: wait for the discovery stage of the sales story. You will have your fair share of time to ask questions that will help you understand the customer and their unique situation. But certainly not in the probing stage—patience is key.

The only way to avoid asking irrelevant questions is to prepare your questions in advance and study them carefully. It may take some trial and error before you know exactly what to ask and when. Limit your probing session to two or three open-ended questions. Conduct pre-call planning and look for information about your account, be it on their website or social media. Set your meeting up for success and avoid asking simple and basic questions.

With the topic of the cloud in mind, let's carefully examine what types of questions to ask to figure out whether you are with the right customer or not. Here is a simple question that would uncover the customer's current situation:

- Where are the servers hosted?

The answer to this question could be one or two of the following:

1- We host our servers in-house/on premises.
2- The servers are on the cloud.
3- The servers are managed from our headquarters in New York.
4- We don't have servers.
5- The servers are in Etisalat's data center.

Here is the dilemma: All of these scenarios must be looked at differently, as there is no one-size-fits-all sales story. Let's assume that I am targeting customers who host their servers in-house. The question is going to help me determine what the next course of action is. If the customer says, for example, that they are on Azure, the discussion will be entirely different. I would not use the sales story that I prepared for clients using in-house servers because the client is already on Azure cloud infrastructure, and my sales story would be irrelevant.

However, if the customer says, "We are hosting our servers in-house," I would use my sales story, which was designed to address this specific target market. You get the idea.

AGREEMENT

Agreement is the third step in Find the Gap stage. After deciding on which sales story to use, the first thing you want to do is to *agree*. Agreement opens up doors to build rapport. We like others to agree with us and usually don't like people who tend to disagree with what we say. Another reason why agreement is important is that you are about to share issues that are relevant to their business. This may trigger resistance, as they will feel attacked. Therefore, agreeing with them will diffuse some of that anger or doubt.

Always, always, always agree with the customer. The customer is more interested in you agreeing with them rather than you being right. The two most powerful words in the English language are "I agree." The two words "I agree" are magic! Just agree with the customer regardless of whether they are right or wrong. It's not precisely those words that get the job done; you can also praise them when they tell you about a certain decision they've made.

Agreement is the road to winning the customer's heart and mind. Let's apply the rule of agreement to the cloud sales story. In your probing stage, the question to the customer was, "Where are the servers hosted?" Let's assume the customer says, "The servers are hosted in-house."

Scenario One: Disagreement

So now that you are aware the customer's servers are hosted in-house, you can reply by saying what you think is true. Let's assume your answer goes something like this: "Hosting the servers in-house is risky. You might lose all of your servers because of a fire or malware attack." Think for a moment; this sounds like a disagreement about how the customer manages their setup. You are indirectly telling the customer that keeping the servers in-house is stupid because they didn't bother to think of all the risks that come with keeping the servers on premises. I know this is not what you meant, but believe me, this is how you will sound, and this is how the customer will hear it.

Scenario Two: Agreement

Let's look at the agreement scenario and see how it goes. You ask the customer the same question. Where are the servers hosted? The customer replies by saying that the servers are hosted in-house. Here is how your agreement comes into play: "Smart choice. Hosting your servers in-house ensures you have all the control." Here, you indirectly agree with the customer's decision. It gives the impression that you are with the customer and stand by them, whether they are right or wrong.

You have to always agree with the customer regardless of them being right or wrong. First agree, then comment. Practice the rule of agreement on your customers and notice how they react. More often than not, the client will be open to any discussion, and you will be more likable.

POWER STATEMENT

The *power statement* is the fourth step in the Find the Gap stage. The power statement serves two purposes. First, it provides a ton of credibility to your argument. Not all RMs have a strong background on a particular subject they intend to discuss with the customer in detail. Their position is maybe weak because, most likely, the customer knows more than they do. So how do you strengthen your position? It is quite straightforward: Using a power statement will put you in a favorable position and will enable you to communicate a piece of information that may not be aligned with your background.

The second purpose of the power statement is to provide a heads-up to the customer on the challenges faced by other customers in that particular industry. Sometimes the customers are not aware of these issues; therefore, the power statement is a practical way to highlight these issues. But also remember not to prolong the exposition of the issues if the customer gives the impression that he is aware of that particular issue.

You can use many forms of the power statements, and here are some examples:

- "According to industry experts . . ." (then state the challenge)
- "As per subject matter experts . . ." (then state the challenge)
- "According to Gartner . . ." (then state the challenge)
- "As per HBR . . ." (then state the challenge)

Here is how it plays out:

Salesperson: Subject matter experts say that there are many challenges linked with hosting the servers in-house, for example:

- Security threats
- Business continuity concerns (Internet disconnection/power disruption, fire breakout, and hardware failure)
- Budget and resource constraints

Coming back to the cloud sales story, after probing and agreement, the discussion continues. In this example, I would like to deliver my sales story without a power statement. Let's look at how the conversation goes.

Scenario 1: No power statement used

RM: Where are the servers hosted?

Customer: The servers are hosted in-house.

RM: Yes, I have had many customers in your industry who host their servers in-house. And I find that there are many risks associated with having the servers in-house. There could be business continuity issues or malware attacks.

The customer is unsettled and unwilling to listen because this piece of information is coming from the RM, who is not exactly an authority on the subject matter.

Now let's change the scenario to where the RM uses a power statement and notice the difference.

Scenario 2: Power statement used

RM: Where are the servers hosted?

Customer: They are hosted in-house.

RM: I agree with you, many of our customers in your industry host their servers in-house. However, as per industry experts, there are many challenges associated with hosting the servers in-house; there could be business disruptions or security threats.

The customer is willing to listen and will be more receptive, as the RM is backing up what he or she said with the opinion of industry experts.

Always use a power statement to brace what you say. It will, without a doubt, strengthen your position and will enable you to share your thoughts as well.

Ask – engage the customer

Asking provocative questions throughout the discussion is a way to actively engage the customer. Engaging the customer in the conversation will help uncover all the initial issues. When you deliver your power statement and highlight the problems other customers face, ask the customer if they have experienced similar issues before. If the answer is yes, this is a good place to start, as you know precisely what kind of challenges they are going through. They could also highlight some other problems that were not part of your list. The initial identification of the problems will act as a reference when we get to the discovery part of the sales story.

The second thing you want to know is if they have ever thought of addressing these problems. Why is this important? They will talk about their attempts to solve these problems, if any. Then you can pick up the discussion from where they leave it.

DISCOVERY

All of the previous steps were preliminary to the discovery stage. Discovery is the most important stage in the sales story. In fact, the entire sales framework depends on how well the discovery stage is managed. By now, you know that closing happens in this stage, not the last stage. You must spend a considerable amount of time trying to understand more about the customer and their unique situation.

Keenan, the author of *Gap Selling*, shares a framework that is interesting and straight to the point. He talks about how important it is to identify the current state of the customer versus the future state of the customer.

The discovery stage is divided into two parts: discovery #1 and discovery #2. Discovery #1 tackles the current state of the customer by identifying the existing problems, the impact of these problems on the customer's business, and the root cause of the gap.

Discovery #2 is all about exploring the future state of the customer with all the problems addressed and the opportunities available for the customer to take advantage of. Then it discusses the positive impact of these opportunities on the customer's business. The last part is quantifying the positive impact and the negative impact if the status quo prevails.

Discovery #1: Current State of the Customer:

There are three critical elements to uncover in discovery #1:

1- Identify the problems.

2- Evaluate the impact of the problems.

3- Identify the root cause of the problems.

1- Identify the problems.

As stated earlier, there is a high likelihood of the client not being aware that a gap exists. If they were aware, they would have fixed it before you even highlighted it. Identifying the problems is difficult, but getting the customer to agree that there is a problem is the most challenging part of the sales story. I know it is hard. That is why underperformers let excuses get in the way and never show the reality to the customer because it entails a massive amount of action to convince the customer that there is a gap that needs to be bridged for the betterment of their company.

Uncovering the problems by engaging with the customer is a powerful exercise, and it is worth every minute you spend on the lead, as it gets you closer to creating a qualified opportunity. As the client engages in the discussion, they will feel that they are coming up with the analysis themselves, and thus you will get their buy-in.

Provide the customer hints about the problems other customers face and ask if they are experiencing similar issues. Setting the right expectations before engaging the customer with the problem identification exercise is essential partly because they do not know what your goals are.

First, evaluate common challenges with them and see if they are relevant to their business. The customer will feel comfortable because you are indirectly informing them that you are not going to offer any solution. Rather, you are going to work with them to address the issues if they are relevant to their business. The second thing is the timing: If the customer says that it is not the right time to carry on with the activity, schedule it for next week. Avoid shooting straight questions at them and tell them what you are going to do. It goes like this:

> **RM:** I would like to do a little activity with you to show you the challenges other customers in your industry face and the impact of these issues on their business. Then you and I will

evaluate if these challenges are relevant to your business or not. Are you open to doing that?

Customer: Yes, go ahead.

RM: Industry experts say that companies in your industry are facing many challenges when it comes to managing on-premises servers: things like business continuity, security, scalability, dependence on a third party, and slow service deployment. Are these challenges relevant to your business?

(Let the information sink in; the customer may not be aware of these issues. Give them a few seconds to think and respond. If they say, "Yes, some of these issues are relevant to our business," BINGO, you are on the right track and getting closer to creating a qualified opportunity. If they say, "We don't feel these concerns are relevant to our business," ask if they can think of any other challenges they face today pertaining to the infrastructure.)

Customer: Yeah, business continuity seems to keep us up at night, and we need to think about a way to address it.

RM: Alright, what about other aspects of the business, like scalability, slow-to-market deployment, or security?

Customer: Security seems to be the second concern. It is becoming hard to manage all the security components, especially looking at how we are growing.

RM: If I get you correctly, here are the concerns you would like to address: business continuity and the security aspect of the business. OK, let's figure out the impact of these issues on your business.

Problem Identification Chart:

Identify problems	Evaluate impact	Identify root cause
- Security		
- Business Continuity		
- Scalability		
- Slow deployment to market		
- Operation and annual maintenance costs		
- Overdependence on third party		

(Great, you have identified two challenges the customer is experiencing. This does not mean you uncovered all the gaps. There are a few challenges the customer does not seem to know about—for example, scalability or slow deployment to market. You can address any other issues you think the customer is unaware of when you come to the Identify the Impact *part of the discovery stage.)*

2- Identify the impact of the problems.

When you engage the customer in impact-evaluation activity, make the discussion interesting by asking the customer to identify the impact of one issue. Then you identify the effects of another, especially the ones that are relatively unknown. If they are not aware of a problem, how will they let you know its impact? This is your chance to highlight it to them and make them aware of the existence of these gaps that they can't see or think of.

Evaluate the impact of the problems by asking provocative questions like the following: How significant will the impact be if there is a malware attack? How much do you think it will cost the company? For how long do you think the company will shut down if a fire breaks out in the data center or the building?

The discussion with the customer continues:

> **RM:** I agree. Many customers in your industry have the same challenges. What could be the impact of these unforeseen events on your business's continuity, for example, if there is Internet disconnection or power disruption or a fire in the building? How is that going to impact your business?
>
> **Customer**: I am not sure. I guess the impact will be significant. We can't handle that.
>
> **RM:** Anything you could think of?
>
> **Customer:** Maybe the risk of power disruption or fire breakout will lead to data loss and loss of capital.
>
> **RM:** Can we quantify it?
>
> **Customer:** If my servers are down for one week, I guess the impact will be anything between $200K and $500K.
>
> **RM**: I agree with you. This has been the case with other customers as well. You know, Ameer, other clients also suggest that outsourcing the infrastructure to a third party is considered a risk because the third party could shut down your business at any time. This incident happened with one of the accounts I manage. They were in trouble because the third party had just left the country with no proper handover. Another incident happened with another customer of mine, where the third party was holding them hostage and was refusing to hand over the credentials. Do you think something like this could occur?

Customer: Yeah, possibly.

RM: Okay, you mentioned another area of concern, which is security. What do you think the impact will be if there is a malware attack?

Customer: If anything like that happens, we definitely won't be able to tolerate any financial impact, downtime, or damage to our brand.

RM: I agree. It is a big concern. Have you thought of any financial impact if a malware attack happens?

Customer: Maybe another $200K for ransomware.

RM: Yes, and sometimes it is even more. One of the customers I manage was hacked, and the attacker was asking for $600K. The issue is not with the money. They paid, but when they got their data back, half of the information was encrypted.

Customer: That is sad.

(Notice that the salesperson shared multiple case studies of other customers as the discussion continued. The customer knew that the impact would be significant, but they didn't yet have a comprehensive survey of the total cost versus the benefit. The situation will get serious with cost/benefit analysis.)

3- **Identify the root cause.**

RM: Okay, I get that. In your opinion, what could be the root cause of these issues?

Customer: I guess having the servers in-house.

RM: True. Is there any plan to address these concerns?

(Notice the discussion between the RM and the customer. The RM was

intentionally trying to get the customer to answer all the questions by themselves because the RM knows that it is the only way to get the customer's buy-in. If they arrive at a conclusion themselves, they will definitely be in. Your role is simply to coach the customer and steer the discussion to make it look like they are addressing the problems all by themselves.)

The problem-identification and impact-evaluation exercises with the customer can be captured in a table (illustrated below) for future reference. Email this table to customers after your discussion for better clarity.

Impact Identification Chart

Identify problems	Evaluate impact	Identify root cause
- Security - Business continuity - Scalability - Slow deployment to market - Operation and annual maintenance costs - Overdependence on third party	- Risk of malware attack - Risk of power disconnection - Risk of Internet disconnection - Risk of fire breakout - Loss of data - Loss of money - Loss of the entire data center - High cost - High maintenance - Slow deployment to market	- On-premises hosting

The above is just an example, and it is not comprehensive in any way. Conduct a brainstorming session with your colleagues to identify all the gaps the clients could face in a particular industry. The customer will share more information about their current situation if you ask the right provocative questions.

Think about it. If you were a business owner and a salesperson approached you with all the problems that your business could be exposed to, wouldn't it make sense to give it a thought and check if these problems were real? If they were, would you assess the impact and see the damage these problems could cause? I am optimistic that this will always be the case—unless the owner doesn't care about the business.

Discovery #2: The Future State of the Customer:

The future state comes after the discovery #1 (current state of the customer). It is the right time to demonstrate to the customer how you will help them achieve better results in the future. The discussion continues:

> **RM:** Great, I would like to share with you the experience of other customers after moving to the cloud.
>
> First, they secured business continuity, no risk of malware attack, no risk of power disconnection, etc. Second, they reduced cost and are in control of their data. Third, they optimized their operations by achieving faster deployment to market with little resources and can scale up and down when the situation demands.
>
> **Customer:** Interesting!
>
> **RM:** Let's do a little activity together to quantify the impact and then decide whether it makes sense to go ahead or not.

(When demonstrating the future state, list all the opportunities that can be derived from the solution and discuss the positive impact on the customer's business. Quantifying the positive impact will speed up the decision-making process.)

There are three elements to address in discovery #2 in the future state of the customer:

- Identify opportunities.

- Evaluate positive impact.
- Quantify positive impact.

Opportunity Identification Chart

Identify opportunities	Evaluate positive impact	Quantify positive impact
- Little or no management is required - No third-party dependency - Risk-free environment - Guaranteed business continuity - Faster deployment - Reduce cost	- No business disruption - No risk of downtime - No security threats - Fast deployment - Cost savings	- Refer to cost/benefit analysis

Sometimes, the positive impact value may not be evident immediately, and would not be quantified straight away. However, try to be as realistic as possible. To illustrate the impact, share a case study of a company whose size and business are similar to the one you are engaged with.

COST/BENEFIT ANALYSIS

A cost/benefit analysis or total cost of ownership (TCO) is a potent exercise and a must-do if you want to close a deal. It is a way to show the customer their current spend versus future spend, something they have never done before. This exercise will be an eye-opener, as it brings clarity to the discussion. The decision-making process will be simple, easy, and, most importantly, quick. After all, decision-makers are interested in looking at numbers. Therefore, this activity is of paramount importance. You can't skip it if you want to close more deals at the price you want.

Because the cost/benefit analysis activity takes time, it can be carried out in the second meeting with the customer. In your first meeting with the customer and after the gap analysis, capture the requirements you need to prepare for the TCO activity. If you can do both the gap analysis and cost/benefit analysis in one sitting, go right ahead. But for the best results, I recommend that you separate the two activities.

Conducting the cost/benefit analysis with the customer will take twenty to thirty minutes. It is essential to set expectations and prepare the customer's mind before jumping into the discussion. The customer should understand what you are up to because you will be asking many questions. Here is an example:

> **RM:** There is an opportunity for you to save on costs and be in a risk-free environment. I would like to do a little activity with you to show you exactly what I mean. Are you open to it? *(Setting expectations at every stage is important.)*
>
> **Customer:** Yes, go ahead.
>
> **RM:** I will list the current setup in one column along with the cost and list the proposed setup along with its cost. At the end, and after seeing the total cost for both scenarios, we can decide whether to go forward or not. (*The customer will definitely agree because you are very clear on what you want to do.*)

When the product is simple, conducting a cost/benefit analysis in detail is not necessary. It really depends on the complexity of the solution you sell. You are the best judge. To get this activity right, you need to ask more about the customer's current setup, capture all the information, and never miss anything. The customer may forget one component or the other. Just pay attention and ask.

The discussion goes on:

RM: How many racks do you have, and what kind of servers do you manage?

Customer: I have one rack and have the following servers:

- Active directory
- Firewall
- Exchange server
- Application server
- Database server
- Accounting server

RM: How many employees do you have?

Customer: We have thirty employees.

RM: Great, let's do the cost/benefit analysis and see if our product can be the right fit for you.

(Be careful here; the customer may forget one component of the solution or another. Your role is to correct them. For example, if they don't mention a firewall or active directory, you should remind them. You have to get all the servers and other equipment listed down to do a comprehensive exercise.)

Cost-Benefit Analysis Example:

Current Setup	Current Cost	Proposed Solution	Proposed Cost – 30 Users
Active directory	$2,000	Active directory on SaaS	30×25 = $750
Firewall		Security solution	30×25 = $750
Exchange server		O365	30×20 = $600
Accounting server		SAGE	$1,000 (10 licenses)
Share point server		Inclusive with O365	
Database server		Goes to virtual machine	$2,000
Application server		Goes to virtual machine	$2,000
Third-party charges	$3,000	Third party will manage only the virtual machines – thus, their scoop will be reduced by 50%	$1,500
Utility bill	$3,000	Since all servers will move out of the office, there is no utility bill for the servers	0
Human resource cost – two people	$10,000	Only one is needed; the other one can be utilized somewhere else in the company	$5,000
Risk-free environment – opportunity cost	$3,000	Customer will be in a risk-free environment	0
Amortization cost over five years	$700	No need to invest in hardware in the future	0
Total	**$21,700**		**$12,700**

The above is just an example; numbers will change depending on the customer and the situation.

Providing this kind of clarity to the customer will help in closing the deal, especially when you present such data to the decision-makers. They will be able to decide based on facts, as opposed to assumptions. Informing the customer that a cloud solution will reduce costs or place them in a safer environment won't help much. As long as the numbers are not visible to them, decision-making will be quite complex. I know it is time-consuming and challenging. Only top performers go through it because they understand the chance of winning the client's business is slim to none without the TCO or cost/benefits analysis activity.

CREATE A SENSE OF URGENCY

Creating a sense of urgency is the sixth step in the Find the Gap stage. On the pain scale of 1 to 10, how do you rate the pain of the customer? The greater the pain, the more urgent it becomes to fix the problem. The impact of the problems on the customer's business determines the level of pain. If the customer doesn't feel pain for any reason, go back to the discovery phase and do it all over again. There is a big chance you missed something, or the customer didn't understand your reasoning. Customers with a 1 on the pain scale should not get into your pipeline and should never divert your focus and attention from the clients with a 6 or above.

You can create a strong sense of urgency by identifying all the problems correctly, stressing the impact of the problems on their business, and quantifying the impact in terms of value. Sharing an incident to highlight what happened with other customers is another powerful exercise to create a sense of urgency. A lot of us panic and act only if an unpleasant incident occurs to somebody else. We try our best to avoid such events happening to us. When we hear that someone got a malware attack and paid a ransom, we freak out and try to do something about it. When we hear that a fire broke out last week in the neighborhood, we run to protect ourselves from any unforeseen incidents. This is who we are, and this is how we behave. Pick a suitable case study and use it to create a sense of urgency.

STAKEHOLDER ENGAGEMENT

The seventh step in the Find the Gap stage is stakeholder engagement. In part two of this book, we discussed the importance of building meaningful relationships with our customers well in advance. We also discussed how building relationships will serve us well when the right time comes. By now, you know that a meaningful relationship is all about getting to know everybody in the account, starting with the CEO, CIO, and other key stakeholders, and striving to have a strong bond that is hard for anyone to break. Ideally, engaging the key stakeholders should be at the beginning of the discussion, but if your point of contact does not agree to involve other stakeholders until you run the material by him or her, fine, do that. However, after your gap analysis and cost/benefit analysis, you must involve and get connected to key stakeholders who will eventually sign on the dotted line.

The second round of discussion with the decision-makers will be easier, since the discovery part is done. You will only be presenting the facts. If you leave it to your point of contact to deliver the message to the decision-makers, there is a high probability that he or she won't deliver it the way you would. Passing up the message yourself will have two benefits: First, you will show the decision-makers that you care and are doing your best to find solutions to the existing problems, and second, you will ensure the right message reaches the right stakeholders. Most importantly, you don't want to level up to the decision-makers when your point of contact doesn't agree to go with your solution.

SUMMARIZE THE GAP

Okay, I must admit, identifying the gaps and getting the customer to agree that there is a gap is tricky and time-consuming. Unfortunately, there is no shortcut to selling—every step in the process matters. Top performers put in the time and effort to do what it takes because they know the deal is closed in the discovery part of the sales story, not the last stage of the sales process.

The last stage of Find the Gap is about summarizing the gaps you have identified with the customer and getting their agreement on the existence of the gaps. If the customer disagrees, go back to the discovery part and do it all over again. Perhaps they didn't understand your point of view and still feel there are no problems to fix. If this is the case, moving to the Bridge the Gap part of the sales story doesn't make sense. After all, there can't be solutions if you don't clearly identify the problems and the impact of these problems on the customer's business. On the other hand, if the customer agrees that there is an issue to solve, you have done a brilliant job, and this opportunity deserves to be in your pipeline. You are now ready to bridge the gap.

Phew! This was long, wasn't it? As I mentioned earlier, the discovery part is the most challenging part of the sales story. Average salespeople don't invest the time to do things right. They just want to take shortcuts and get to a point where they are comfortable discussing the product and highlighting its features. Here is a reality check: If you desire to be in the elite category, you must religiously go through the Find the Gap stage. You could skip all of these steps and focus on your product, but chances are that the decision-making process will be lengthier and more difficult.

Let's summarize what we have covered so far in the Find the Gap part of the sales story before moving to Bridge the Gap:

- Setting expectations
- Probing
- Agreement
- Power statement
- Discovery
- Creating a sense of urgency
- Engaging the stakeholders
- Summarizing the gap

SALES STORY P #2: BRIDGE THE GAP

Find the Gap stage was all about the customer and their concerns. Now it is time to focus on you and your solutions. As I mentioned earlier, part two of the sales story should never precede part one. It is surprising when average RMs jump to the solution and start talking about how great, fantastic, and affordable the product is. Guys, hold your horses. The customer doesn't care about your product or service. The customer first wants to know what's in it for them.

Let's assume that you have succeeded in highlighting all the problems that impact the customer's business, and the customer somehow agrees that these problems exist. Now it is time to share your solution and explain the value your product can offer and ultimately bridge the gap.

SOLUTION/OFFERING

By now, the idea is sold to the customer, and the deal is closed even before discussing the offering. Explaining the solution is just a byproduct of doing the Find the Gap stage right. The discussion will continue, and the relationship manager will mainly focus on the product and show how the gaps will be bridged.

> **RM:** Earlier, we identified the challenges that are relevant to your business when it comes to hosting the servers in-house, which are:

- Business continuity issues;
- Security concerns;
- Dependence on a third party;
- Scalability;
- Slow deployment of services; and
- Cost.

With our solution, we will make sure none of these challenges occur:

1- Business continuity is a top priority for us, and here is how we ensure zero downtime:

   a. We provide five layers of power redundancy.

   b. We provide multiple layers of Internet redundancy.

   c. Our certified data center buildings are stand-alone, and we have strong fire-suppression systems.

d. We provide multiple layers of firewall to protect the virtual machines from any malware attacks.

e. We provide high availability of the virtual machine; if the hosted VM is down, your services will be automatically moved to another VM.

2- Eliminate overdependence on third parties by enabling your team to manage the infrastructure themselves through an easy-to-use portal.

3- Help faster deployment to market by providing resources when and as needed.

4- Achieve cost optimization by scaling up and down as per the business requirement. We also have a pay-as-you-go model.

Customer: Interesting, can you show me how it works?

RM: Sure, let me take you through the demo of the product.

DEMO

There is an old adage that says, "Seeing is believing." The product demo is proof that it does what it says. The customer gets to know how the product's features will solve their existing problems and achieve the desired outcome.

Having the ability to see and feel the product is more appealing to clients than simply talking about it. A quick demo of the product will encourage the client to have a sense of ownership. That is why car dealers try their best to get the customer to test drive. The demonstration also helps clear all the misconceptions or confusion the customer might have about the product.

When doing the product demo for the customer, try to tailor your approach to focus on the product's features that will address the identified gaps. Don't underestimate the product demo; it is the best tool you can use. It will definitely help in closing the deal and winning the customer's business.

PRICE OF THE PRODUCT

The price of the product comes last. Justifying the price is easy when the customer sees value. If the price is the first thing the RM talks about, any price will seem high to the customer. Do the first part right, and trust me, the customer will pay any price to bridge the identified gaps, especially if the gaps are significant. On the other hand, the underperformers discount the price of their product heavily and let the margin go because they are unable to identify the gaps, get the customer to agree that there are gaps, create a sense of urgency, and articulate the value of their product.

SALES STORY P #3: DIFFERENTIATION

There are three different types of salespeople. The first type does whatever it takes to understand the customer first, finds the gaps, and then proposes a solution. The second type jumps straight to the solution and starts pitching without understanding the customer's unique requirements. Unfortunately, the third type starts the sales discussion with differentiation. They talk about how big their company is and how long they have been in the market, forgetting that the client does not care about their company or product in the early stages of the sales cycle.

Informing the customer that your company has been in the market for the last twenty years is not wrong, but not when your first task is to identify the gaps. If you still feel that sharing such information is necessary, share a link to your company's website. If the customer is interested in learning more, they will do it in their own free time. In fact, they would have Googled your company and already know everything about you.

The differentiation stage of the sales story is all about showing how our solution is better than the competition's offering. Differentiation becomes critical and a key deciding factor if the solution is straightforward. The customer evaluates how every vendor or supplier is different from one another. In specific scenarios, especially when the customer knows about the gaps they desire to bridge, differentiation becomes the only way to win the customer's business. If this is the case, the RM takes a shortcut, passes all the stages, and goes to the differentiation part of the sales story. Spending time identifying the business gaps may not be necessary because this activity was carried out by someone else or the customer themselves. However, the RM should try to find a different type of problem. Work with the customer to identify all the shortcomings they are experiencing with the current or potential vendors and address them. For example, if the customer points out that the current vendor's support system is ineffective, we know the customer is concerned about support, and providing superior support could be one way to win their business.

The differentiators could be about the company, product, support system, price, or customer experience. What are your company's strengths?

1- Company's reputation/brand

2- Company's financial strength

3- Company's values

4- Company's proximity

5- Product reliability

6- Product features

7- Product uniqueness

8- Product novelty

9- Pre-delivery support

10- Delivery process

11- Post-delivery support

12- Price versus value

13- Price structure—one-time charge versus monthly charge

14- Price during the life cycle of the product

15- Customer experience

16- Customer loyalty

While a differentiated product is a cornerstone to winning the deal, there is another angle to differentiation: you. Establishing trust and building a meaningful relationship with your client is what separates you from the rest of the competitors. Being different is entirely within your control—it doesn't need a budget or resources. Four main things will differentiate you from your competitors:

1- Building a meaningful relationship that is solely based on caring, placing the customer's interests before yours.

2- Being genuinely interested in solving their problems and co-creating new possibilities that never existed before.

3- Being responsive and attentive and taking extreme ownership of the deal from start to finish.

4- Delivering an experience that impresses the client and creates an impact for a long-lasting relationship.

Combining the four differentiators along with the other differentiators your company provides will enable you to close the deal at the price you want!

Bringing Objections to the Surface:

We all know that at a certain point in the sales process, the customer will object or reject the solution for one reason or the other. How do we handle it?

There are four scenarios for handling objections:

1- The first scenario is to walk away without understanding the reasons your customer is not interested in buying your solution. This is the worst thing you could do to yourself.

2- The second scenario is to understand why the customer is not buying. The customer explains why they are not going with the solution, but you think the reason doesn't make sense. In fact, the opposite is true and that calls for further discovery. Go back to the discovery stage and ensure that the customer understands the problems and its impact on their business.

3- In the third scenario, the customer shares a valid reason for not buying, and you also think the solution is not the perfect fit. The best thing to do is to walk away, as there is no opportunity to capture, at least for now.

4- The fourth scenario is that the customer is not comfortable disclosing any reason for not buying. This is where things get complex. The best thing to do here is to be empathetic, put yourself in the customer's shoes, and try to bring the objections out in the open and begin addressing them.

Let's assume that you have identified an opportunity for a cloud solution. The customer hesitated and eventually said no. They are uninterested and unwilling to share the reason with you. You might bring up the objection that you feel is logical. It is usually the case with a lot of businesses that are not ready to invest their time and money into overhauling the status quo. In that case, you could say something like this:

- o John, since your company has not done something like this before, I am guessing you might be wondering if the solution is reliable. Am I reading this correctly?
- o John, I get the feeling that changing the supplier might be a hassle as they are currently managing most of your network. Am I reading this situation correctly?
- o John, if I were you, I would also be thinking that changing my infrastructure will take time and effort. It is better to keep everything as is for the moment. Am I reading the situation correctly?

Bringing the objection out in the open will allow you to address it. It will make way for your point of contact to have a meeting with internal stakeholders, which will eventually help you realize your opportunity. Sometimes, the customer will resist, but they may not know exactly what prevents them from going with the solution.

SALES STORY RECAP

Okay, we have come to the end of the sales story. Here is a recap of what we have done. We got into a discussion with the customer with one objective in mind: finding the gap. The first thing we did was set the right expectations for the meeting. Next, we asked probing questions to figure out whether to push forward with the discussion or retreat. Then, we agreed with the customer, regardless of him or her being right or wrong, to build likability and put the customer at ease, and to let them save face because we shared a few problems they were not aware of, or maybe they were, but they didn't do anything to fix them. After that, we used a power statement to deliver tons of credibility by referring to a well-known authority, like Gartner or industry experts.

Then we moved to the most crucial part of the sales story, which is the discovery phase or gap analysis. We spent a considerable amount of time trying to understand the customer's current state by identifying the problems and the impact of these problems on their business as well as the root cause. Then we moved to the future state of the customer and identified the available opportunities for the customer to leverage. We also quantified the impact to have a better clarity and understand the value our solution provides.

The discussion continued. We created a sense of urgency by sharing multiple case studies. Then we engaged the customer in a cost/benefit analysis exercise to clarify the current cost versus the future cost, to make the decision-making process easier and faster. Engaging the stakeholders was necessary after the cost/benefit analysis, and we have summarized the problems to set a clear next step.

We jumped to the second part of the sales story, Bridge the Gap, and talked about the solution and how it would help bridge all the identified gaps. Next, we moved to the demo of the product to showcase what we said the product does, and we focused on the most important benefits related to the customer's needs.

The customer was interested in knowing the price from the early stages of the sales story, but we delayed it until we conveyed our message and showed the proposition the way it should have been shown.

After that, we moved to the third and last part of the sales story, which is the Differentiation. We communicated why they should buy from us. We went into the details and showed the customer how our product is superior to all other products on the market. We also demonstrated our level of expertise to create a lasting impression on the customer and win the deal at the price we want.

The end of the story: "The king killed the witch, and everybody lived happily ever after."

This, in a nutshell, is how ultra-high performers orchestrate the sales story. They don't skip the process and don't rush to closure. Sales takes time, and always remember, if there is no problem, there is no sale. Focus your attention and time on identifying the problems, and work with the customer to find solutions to these problems. It is incredible if the customer realizes the problems themselves because they will be more interested in solving issues they uncover.

Chapter 16

SALES PIPELINE MANAGEMENT

C rafting a compelling sales story leads to building a resilient sales pipeline. The skillset has a direct correlation to your pipeline-building activity. And the idea here is very simple: no skillset, no pipeline.

Let's assume that you have mastered the sales story. Now is the time to shed light on the sales pipeline and the methodologies available to manage all the opportunities you have worked hard to create.

A sales pipeline is the sum of the opportunities created and managed over time by moving them through multiple sales stages until they are closed-won or closed-lost. The sales pipeline predicts the short-term performance and forecasts the future performance of the RM. It's an instant evaluation of not only the performance but also the RM's skillset and productivity.

The Building Blocks of Sales Pipeline Management:

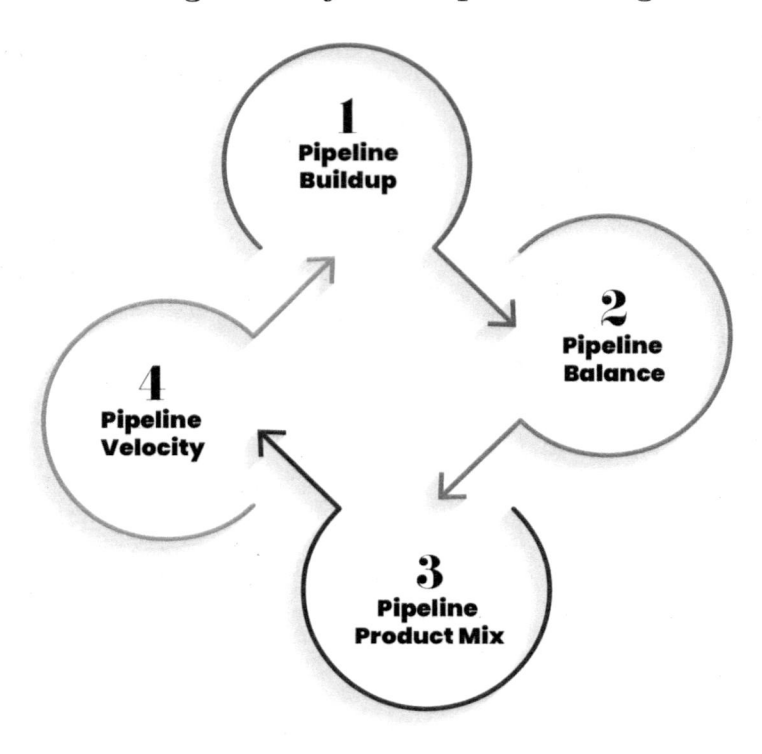

1 Pipeline Buildup

2 Pipeline Balance

3 Pipeline Product Mix

4 Pipeline Velocity

Pipeline building blocks

Chapter 17
PIPELINE BUILDUP

Top performers understand the importance of having a pipeline full of qualified opportunities at any given point in time. Prospecting daily is non-negotiable; they never waste a day, and they are disciplined about it.

Earlier, we discussed the importance of setting low-level and mid-level goals to reach the high-level goals. Defining the daily and weekly numbers around opportunity creation is key to building a healthy pipeline. Prospecting daily leads to a decent pipeline by the end of the month and ultimately a resilient pipeline by the end of the year. Take Sara, for example. She sets a daily opportunity-creation target of $10,000. Let's do a little math and evaluate how healthy her pipeline would be in one year's time if she sticks to her plan. Considering the leave and training days, if she prospects for opportunities worth $10,000 per day, she would have $200,000 worth of pipeline by the end of the month and $2,000,000 worth of pipeline by the end of the year. This is the power of consistency.

Managing an empty pipeline can be a hard task, especially when the underperforming RMs continue to struggle with it as they focus on activities unrelated to sales. They would do much better if they decided to converge their efforts and attention on pipeline-building activities.

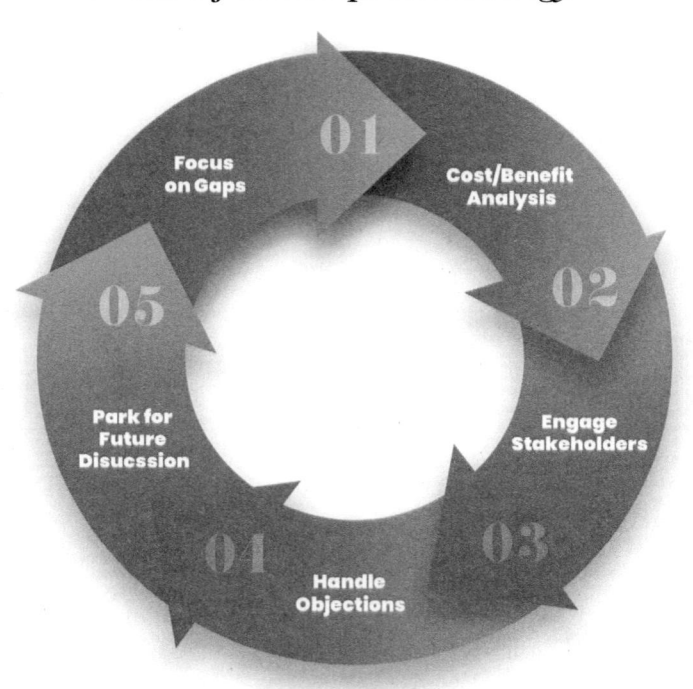

The Fifth Attempt Methodology

- 01 Focus on Gaps
- 02 Cost/Benefit Analysis
- 03 Engage Stakeholders
- 04 Handle Objections
- 05 Park for Future Disucssion

Sales is rarely easy, and it's not like the moment you pick up the phone and prospect, the customer wants the product and finds a nice spot in your pipeline. If you thought this is the case, maybe it is time to wake up and face the brutal reality of sales.

Sales is complex, and only elite sales professionals show great performance month in and month out. Success requires a strong mindset that is disciplined and persistent. These are the vital traits that motivate and propel you forward despite all the challenges and objections thrown at you every day in sales.

Have you ever seen a kid who didn't get what he or she wanted on the first try? I know I have. I have kids, and I have observed their reactions after the first rejection they get from me. After the first no, they go away and quickly come back with a different approach. I stand my ground and say no again. The same scenario continues three, four, five, six times, and guess what? I ultimately say yes to whatever they want. The customer is no different; they will say yes if they think you have value to offer. However, don't be sad about it—the first response will invariably be a no.

I am not advocating that we should be kids in the way we approach customers. However, there is a better and structured way of taking charge of your emotions when it comes to prospecting.

Richard Fenton, the author of *Go for No*, suggests that 60 percent of customers will say yes after the fifth round of discussion. How many attempts do you make to create an opportunity? It's not about how many attempts per se, but rather your approach to creating opportunities. It could go for five, six, and sometimes ten rounds of discussion. However, if you adopt the correct methodology, you don't need to do ten rounds. You can be productive by creating opportunities with a high probability of closure and fewer rounds of discussion.

Do not rush to talk about your product. You will end up sounding irrelevant to your prospect. Instead, you should focus on two critical elements of closing, both of which are found in the Find the Gap stage of the sales process.

The first element is discovery/gap analysis, and the second is cost/benefit analysis. To get the most out of the activity, the salesperson must actively engage the customer in the discussion. There is no point in moving forward if the customer is disengaged. Building interest and managing the customer's expectations happens in the previous stage in the sales process. I know you are pressed for time, and you want to put it all out there for the customer to evaluate and for you to deliver your message in one go. Do not do it. Creating opportunities requires time. First, be patient, and second, be structured. The discovery/gap analysis must be an integral part of your first round of discussion, and the cost/benefit analysis should take place in the second meeting with the client. Your third round is about engaging the right stakeholders to present the findings. The fourth and fifth rounds are for handling objections and closing, or parking the opportunity for future evaluation.

Average salespeople go to the market unprepared. They approach the wrong customers time and time again. They give up after the first round of discussion and eventually complain that no one is buying and the economy is terrible. Let me tell you something: the economy is not bad, because the top performers are always closing regardless of the time of the year. Maybe your mindset and skillset need to change.

Let's unpack the model. Before we do that, it is worth mentioning that, for specific scenarios, you could combine both the discovery/gap analysis and cost/benefit analysis in one meeting. I will leave it for you to decide, depending on how complex your solution is.

Round One—Focus on Gaps:

It is the first encounter with the customer. I assume by now you know the default answer already. In the first attempt, your primary goal is to do the gap analysis with the customer. Understand the customer well and tailor your message to address their needs. The one-size-fits-all approach doesn't work in business sales since every customer is unique in nature—and so should be your approach to market. As explained in the sales story, a comprehensive and engaging discovery is imperative to register the opportunity in your pipeline.

Identifying and quantifying the impact is essential to bring clarity to the discussion. More often than not, the customer will be indecisive; they will evaluate the information you revealed. If done correctly, the customer will be surprised by the data and will definitely think about it.

Many customers, however, try to protect themselves. The default answer will invariably be a no. Believe it or not, the first no doesn't really mean no. It probably means, "Try something different," or, "I don't get you." It is important to understand why the customer says no. Look at the reasons and evaluate whether it makes sense to go back to the customer or not.

Going to the next round of discussion depends on how well the gap analysis was conducted. If you believe the customer realizes the impact of the problem on their business and still doesn't want to go with the solution, and their reasoning is valid, it is wise to focus your time and energy on other deals that have a high probability of closure.

It is a fine line; only you can decide where it gets drawn. Once the gaps are analyzed and the customer agrees they are somehow relevant, you are ready to go to the next round of discussion. Make sure you gather all the information you need to prepare for the second round, such as their current setup and cost.

Round Two—Focus on Cost/Benefit Analysis:

This is a critical session with the customer. In the first round, you have worked with the customer to uncover all the underlying issues and the probable impact of these issues on their business. Now it is time to work on the second most crucial aspect of the Find the Gap stage, i.e., the cost/benefit analysis or TCO (total cost of ownership), discussed in chapter 15. Conducting the cost/benefit analysis will bring clarity to the discussion and will fast-track the decision-making process. Get yourself closer to creating an opportunity with a high probability of closure by showing the customer what they are currently paying versus what they will pay in the future. Clearly demonstrate the benefits they could get by moving to your solution in terms of monetary value, improving business processes, or enhancing the customer experience. I know it is hard, but do not skip it.

There is a possibility that the customer will throw another objection at you. Understand their concerns and try to discover why they are not convinced with the solution. There is a chance that they did not get your point of view. It is wise to get the customer to see the big picture. You should know what entices the customer to consider your solution, as you know more about the customer than you did in the first round of discussion.

Round Three—Engage the Stakeholders:

Let's assume that the first two rounds of discussion are managed well, and the customer is convinced. Great news, the heavy lifting of gap analysis and cost/benefit analysis has been completed with the point of contact. It is the right time to involve the other stakeholders in the discussion to present the findings, which includes explaining the identified gaps and elaborating on the cost/benefit analysis outcome. Every line item should have a dollar sign attached to it. This is exactly how decision-makers would like you to present the findings. You must take the lead to explain why they should go with your solution and not the competition's. Manage your emotions and don't leave it to your point of contact to present the findings. They won't be able to deliver the message the way you would.

Notice that we are still in the first stage of the sales process, which is Finding the Gap. You cannot pass this stage unless you get the customer's consent that there is a problem to address or an opportunity to capture.

If the first three rounds of discussion are done the right way, the deal is likely to close. All subsequent meetings you will have with the customer are about capturing the requirements to prepare for the delivery of the project. However, if the customer objects, get yourself ready for the fourth round.

Round Four—Handling Objections:

There are two scenarios for handling objections. The first one is straightforward. The customer clearly states why they are not convinced and the reasons for not buying. In these cases, you can address the concern, state your perspective, and clarify any confusion around the solution. The second scenario is not straightforward at all. The customer is not willing to share the reasons for the rejection. They may not be aware of why they are rejecting your solution. If this is the case, it is wise to tune into your emotion and understand what the customer is thinking. Be empathetic, say what the customer is feeling, and bring the objections to the surface to address them. Here is an example:

> **RM:** Ameer, I understand that changing the vendor is a hassle, and you are unsure whether we will be able to deliver as per the contract. Am I reading this correctly?

Ameer: Yes, kind of.

RM: I would like to mention that we have worked with many clients who had the same concern initially. After working with us, they realized that they achieved better results. We are ready to work with you, align our objectives with yours, and achieve outstanding results.

Ameer: Tell me more about it.

Notice that the RM placed himself on the customer's side of the table. He brought the objection to the surface and explained what the client was likely feeling. In order to take away the tension and uncertainty from the customer's mind, the RM shared a case study of another customer who had the same concern and yet achieved remarkable results.

It is likely that the customer will throw another objection at you or simply say no. Prepare yourself for the fifth round, but know exactly what is going on in the customer's mind and pay attention to the details. Check if they are talking to competition, and try to address the concerns as they pop up.

Round Five—Handling Objections or Parking It for Future Evaluation:

Congratulations if you have come this far. It shows that you are persistent and ready to do what it takes to close the deal. The good news is that 60 percent of customers say yes on the fifth attempt. They will thank you for being persistent, as they will be able to see the value of your solution.

This is a challenging round but worth the try, as by now you know a lot more about the customer, and you also know why the customer is not interested in working with you. You have also met with all the stakeholders and explained the solution and the impact of the problems if the status quo prevails. It is important to note that you get more information about the customer and the competition with every round of discussion.

Address the customer's objection from different angles if you are confident that the customer is clear about the problems or the opportunities. There could be a chance that the discovery stage was not conducted thoroughly. Maybe it is worth reminding the customer of all the gaps that will impact their business and highlighting the cost/benefit analysis of the current state versus the future state.

Important Note:

Each round of discussion may consist of multiple meetings. For example, you may need to conduct three meetings with the customer in the gap analysis round and another two sessions in the cost/benefit analysis round.

Chapter 18
PIPELINE BALANCE

It all starts with prospecting and capturing a qualified lead in the pipeline. Top performers are masters at managing their pipeline, and you can be too. They move the leads from the targeted stage to closure by securing multiple commitments from the customer throughout the pipeline journey.

Top sales professionals put in the effort to obtain a pocketful of "yeses" as the opportunity travels from lead generation to closure. These minor consents on the customer's part will eventually drive the lead forward. Every yes gets you closer to the final destination.

Once the lead hits the pipeline, the opportunity goes through multiple sales stages, depending on the buyer process. Like any other thing in life, if it is managed well, success will be your ally; if left unmanaged, you must gear yourself up to face the music.

We all know that sales is about working with the other party to achieve satisfactory results for both involved. Therefore, a one-sided approach will not work. You must collaborate with the client if you want to close the deal.

In his book *The Lost Art of Closing*, Anthony Iannarino discusses the importance of obtaining commitments to push the deal forward. There are nine commitments I want you to focus on so you successfully move the leads from the targeted stage all the way to closure. Top achievers understand the criticality of securing mini-commitments from the customers, including commitment of time, commitment to accept change, commitment to collaborate, commitment to reach consensus, commitment to invest, commitment to review a proposition, commitment to decide, commitment to execute, and finally, commitment to close the deal. They never close prematurely and never skip these steps because they know jumping to closure will eventually stall the deal.

On the other hand, underperformers dump trash in the pipeline, thinking the more extensive the pipeline, the better. They skip all the critical stages and never ask for these commitments from the customer. They don't know that unqualified leads will ultimately impact the balance and the velocity of the pipeline.

Having an empty pipeline is an obvious concern. However, creating opportunities more than what you can handle is not a good strategy either because focusing on everything is as bad as focusing on nothing. Keep the pipeline within a reasonable range. Adding more opportunities without having the bandwidth to advance the existing ones to the next stage will create havoc in your pipeline.

On average, a relationship manager in the telecom industry converts 50 percent of the pipeline by year-end. However, I have seen less than 10 percent, and I have also come across salespeople who nail it at a 70 percent pipeline conversion rate. What is the reason for such disparity between the two groups? You guessed it!

The pipeline is divided into two main broad categories: active pipeline and closed pipeline.

Active Pipeline Comprises the Following Stages:

- Targeted @15% closure probability
- Active @40% closure probability
- Hot @80% closure probability

Closing Pipeline Comprises the Following Stages:

- Submitted @90%, documents are signed, and the deal is in the delivery stage
- Closed @100%, the deal is closed, and billing started
- Lost @0%, the deal is lost

Stage	Targeted	Active	Hot	Submitted	Closed	Lost
Probability of lead closure	15%	40%	80%	90%	100%	0%

Pipeline Stages

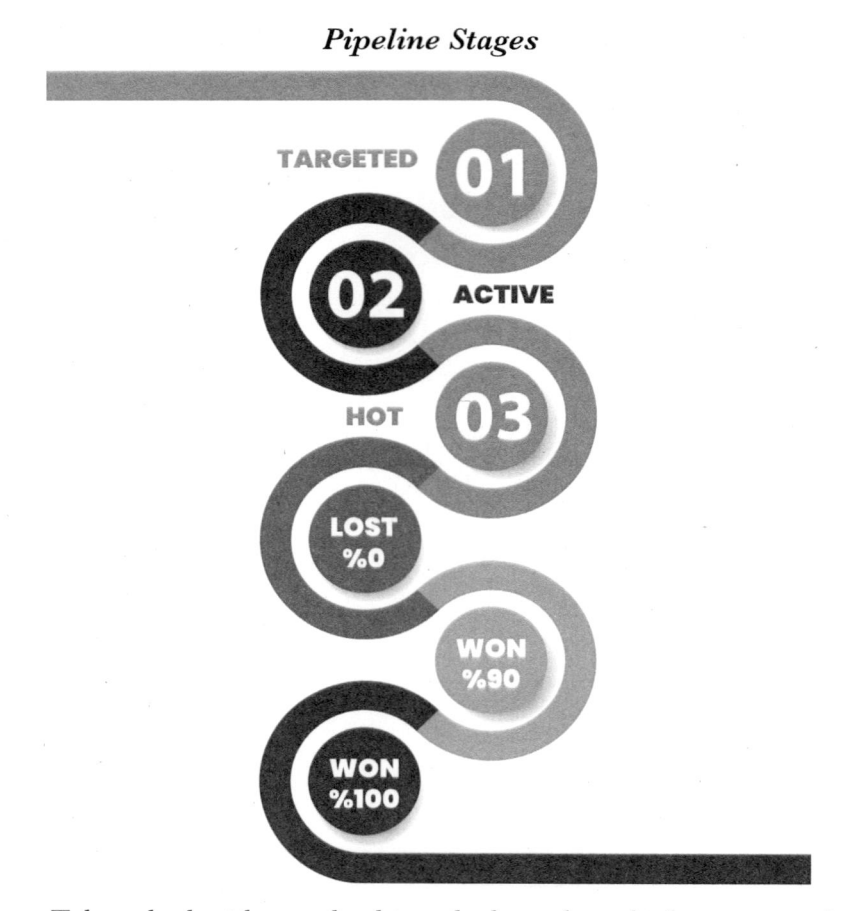

Take a look at how a lead travels through multiple stages in the pipeline, i.e., from the targeted stage to the closed stage.

TARGETED 15 PERCENT

Which lead deserves to be in your pipeline, and how do you know it is a qualified one? Many qualification methods are available in the market, such as BANT (budget, authority, need, and timeline). But this method doesn't work anymore. Think about it; budget is not an issue if the customer wants to address a severe problem impacting their business. They will find the budget to fix the issue. Similarly, you don't sell to a need. You basically identify the problems that are not visible to the clients and address them. Authority and time are manageable because you can get access to the decision-maker, and time is of no concern if the customer sees the impact of the problems on their business.

So how do I qualify a lead? What goes into my pipeline?

To qualify a lead, you need to answer the following questions in the affirmative:

- Is there any problem my solution can solve?
- Is there any opportunity my solution can provide?
- Does the customer agree there is a problem to solve or an opportunity to leverage?

If the answers to all the above questions are in the affirmative, this lead deserves to be in the pipeline, and the likelihood of closing it will be high.

If there is neither a problem to address nor an opportunity to capture, don't waste your time on this lead. It doesn't deserve to be in your pipeline. Find other leads that are worth investing your time in.

Securing commitment from your client throughout the sales journey is imperative to ensure that the lead is on track. The basic commitment you should ask for in the active 15 percent stage is that of the customer's time.

Commitment of Their Time

Commitment of time should be secured throughout the deal from the moment you explore the gap. The customer should be willing to invest their time as much as you are investing your time and efforts. If the customer is disengaged for any reason, there is a possibility they didn't understand the gap. My suggestion is to go back to the first stage and work with the customer to identify and clarify the problems or the opportunities.

ACTIVE 40 PERCENT

Once the lead is captured in your pipeline, the next thing to do is to figure out how to advance it to the active stage. The active stage is the transition from the targeted to the hot stage, and this is where top producers invest most of their time and effort because they know if the active stage is managed well, the deal will make its way to closure. Here are the commitments you should secure from your client in the active stage:

Commitment to Change

For the opportunity to go forward, the client must have a compelling reason to change and look forward to a better future state. This reason is imperative because change is difficult, as it often involves disruption of the client's business. It is essential to know whether the client is ready to make the changes, especially after identifying all the problems and opportunities pertaining to their business.

To ensure the lead is active and the customer is ready to change, ask the customer if all the identified problems are the ones to work on right away. The answer to this question will indicate what to do next. If they say no, ask them to share what is preventing them from going forward. If they give you a convincing reason, it is a crucial piece of information to have early in the process so you can focus on other customers who want to work on the identified problems immediately.

On the other hand, if the customer says yes, you are ready to move the discussion forward, as you have a lead that is likely to be hot. It is vital to ask the client if it is necessary to involve other stakeholders impacted by the change so the client and the RM are aligned and don't get resistance from other stakeholders in the future.

Commitment to Collaborate

The stakeholders must be willing to work with you to solve the problem. Your primary role is to ask questions that will encourage the customer's involvement and participation. Let the client come up with solutions. As a result, they will have greater ownership, as they will have skin in the game. Once they realize the impact of the problems all by themselves, they will feel the idea is theirs and will do anything to defend the solution and relay it to other stakeholders.

Collaboration manifests itself in many aspects—for example, the requirement, design, price, and so on. Remember, you should involve all stakeholders impacted by the change. Talking to your point of contact alone may not help much. Encourage the prospect to collaborate and engage with all stakeholders, and you get yourself a deal that is likely to get closed.

Commitment to Consensus

Building consensus is all about engaging the decision-makers early in the process. You definitely don't want the opportunity to stall because the person you are talking to is not keen on moving the deal forward, despite seeing the value in the change. It is necessary to tackle it early in the discussion, so your contact doesn't feel offended when you call someone else in the organization. You can say something like this:

1- "At some point, we will need to bring in those who will be involved in making the decision . . ."

2- "Who do you think should be part of this discussion?" And . . .

3- "When will it make sense to involve them?"

Their default response may be that they are enough for now, but it is crucial to understand who should be involved to avoid any conflict in the future.

Commitment to Invest

The client must commit to investing energy, effort, and money to bring about the change and address all the challenges. The customer may say we can't afford it as we didn't budget it, but that is not true. They can find the budget if the solution will bring them additional revenue or avert a risk that is likely to occur. If the identified gap is significant, the customer will do anything to work with you to close that gap.

Commitment to Review

Don't be tempted by a request from the customer to simply share the proposal as an email attachment. You have worked very hard on the deal and invested time to put a proposal together; you must get a commitment from the client to review the proposal together. All stakeholders at the client company should be present when you deliver your solution so you can tailor the message to every individual in the decision-making committee. A collaborative review will help you get feedback, make necessary changes, if needed, and address all the concerns that may arise during the process.

HOT 80 PERCENT

Commitment to Decide

The deal finds its way to the hot stage when the customer commits to decide and says the much-awaited word "yes" to your proposition. If the previous commitments were obtained correctly, getting the customer to say yes will not be difficult. It is a default outcome of doing the previous stages right. On the contrary, skipping the prior commitments just to come to this stage of the deal is not an effective strategy. This is the case for many underperforming RMs. They rush to closure without getting the commitment from the customer to change, collaborate, reach consensus, invest, and review the proposal. It will be a challenging task to get the client to say yes on a deal when most of the work is left undone.

Getting the customer to decide is the most straightforward stage of the deal, provided the customer understands the gaps and makes these little commitments to advance the deal in the pipeline.

You are now ready to ask the customer for their business. You could say something like this: "I think we have addressed all the problems, assessed the impact of these problems, and identified all the opportunities that we could leverage on, and we have a good plan in place. All we need right now is the decision maker's signature on the proposal so we can agree on a date to start the work."

Great, since you have delivered your ask, let the customer come back with their thoughts. There could be a possibility that the customer objects because they may need a few amendments to the proposition. That is natural—understand their reasoning and address the amendments to move forward.

SUBMITTED 90 PERCENT

Commitment to Execute

Alright, the customer has signed on the dotted line, and your delivery team is ready to execute the solution. The customer still needs to collaborate with you to get things done, e.g., change the configuration on their devices, move the servers, get the cars to affix your tracking devices, etc. Their system should be compatible with your system. The customer should commit to making all the necessary changes to deliver the solution the way it is designed to be delivered. If for any reason, things aren't working the way they should, the deal could stall, and this is the last thing you want to see.

CLOSED 100 PERCENT

Commitment to Close

Now that the solution has been delivered successfully, the customer is thrilled to be working with a strategic partner who has shouldered the burden from start to finish. You have identified the problem, analyzed the impact, identified the root cause, and worked with the customer to leverage on the identified opportunities and quantify the positive impact of the solution on their business. Not only that, but you have also secured all the necessary commitments to move the deal through your pipeline, i.e., the commitments of time, to change, collaborate, reach consensus, invest, review, decide, execute, and finally, close the deal.

Congratulate yourself for a job well done. Sales is a science. Once you know the rules of the game and do what it takes to close the deal, the outcome will surprise you. Go out there and start applying the rules in your next discussion with your dream clients.

LOST 0 PERCENT

On the flip side, I wish sales was as easy as it seems. Even if you follow all the steps, there might be a chance that your client says no for one reason or other, even if the gap is identified. Don't be sad about it. You have done your part in trying to help the customer, and that's what matters. Sometimes, the client doesn't see value in the proposition and decides to continue with the status quo or go with your competitor. If you have a pipeline full of opportunities, this lost deal should not affect you. I want you to take a deep breath and say: "Who's next?"

BALANCE THE PIPELINE

Pipeline balance indicates how the leads are distributed across the five stages of the pipeline at a particular point in time. A well-balanced pipeline sets you up for success; on the contrary, an imbalanced pipeline will cause you to struggle. The pipeline balance uncovers all the performance issues and shows the skillset gap.

The pipeline balance changes depending on the quarter of the year. Therefore, the first quarter of the year may be different from the last quarter of the year. Planning your time around every stage each day will lead to a well-balanced pipeline. Focusing on pipeline-building activity should be a priority when you notice a decline in the targeted stage. On the other hand, if your active stage is overshooting, you should plan to move the deals to the hot bucket. If you are losing more than 25 percent of your pipeline, you need a serious evaluation of your skillset and the integrity of the leads that go into your pipeline.

To achieve a perfect balance, think about a daily time allocation to the three stages of the pipeline: targeted, active, and hot. Answer the following questions:

- How much time should I allocate to prospecting every week?
- How much time should I allocate to moving leads from targeted to active stage every week?
- How much time should I allocate to moving leads from active to hot stage every week?
- How much time should I allocate to moving leads from hot to closed stage every week?

Mutual agreement between you and your line manager is necessary, and you must always strive to do more. Here is an example of what to aim for every quarter:

Pipeline Balance Matrix

Period	Target	Active	Hot	Closed
Q1	30%	30%	30%	10%
Q2	30%	25%	25%	20%
Q3	25%	25%	20%	30%
Q4	20%	20%	20%	40%

Compare the pipeline balance of Ahmed versus Adel. For the sake of discussion, let's assume that we are in the first quarter of the year, and both of them work for a company in which $250K is considered a healthy pipeline in relation to their respective target of $18K per quarter. The table below is just an example. Discuss with your line manager to agree on numbers that work for you.

AHMED'S PIPELINE BALANCE—Q1 2022 VIEW

Targeted	Active	Hot	Closed	Total
$31,200	$15,600	$2,600	$2,600	$52,000
60%	30%	5%	5%	100%

We can detect many issues with Ahmed's pipeline. The size of the pipeline is the first problem. In this case, $52K is not a healthy pipeline because Ahmed has been part of the team for more than a year. It also shows that Ahmed is busy prospecting but never takes the time to move the leads to the next stage, as it is evident that his targeted stage reached 60 percent. To make matters even worse, 90 percent of his pipeline is at the early stage of the discussion. It is a concern because these leads will eventually get stalled.

It is also noticeable that the hot stage is weak, which will directly impact the closure by the end of the month, and the forecast shows that he will not be able to achieve his quarterly quota. An average RM at this stage should have at least 10 to 15 percent conversion rate, while Ahmed has only 5 percent conversion rate.

Looking at Ahmed's pipeline, we can immediately determine that he is in trouble and needs help. Poor pipeline management is one of the reasons why many salespeople fail. Let's evaluate Adel's pipeline in the table below.

ADEL'S PIPELINE BALANCE—Q1–2022 VIEW

Targeted	Active	Hot	Closed	Total
$88,000	$65,000	$42,000	$26,000	$221,000
40%	29%	19%	12%	100%

Adel's pipeline on the other hand is healthier and well-balanced. First, the size of the pipeline is acceptable based on the company's guidelines. Second, the pipeline is balanced across all stages, from the targeted stage to the closed stage. It is evident that Adel spends a considerable amount of time managing all stages the right way. It is also clear that Adel pays close attention to his pipeline balance and dedicates a specific amount of time every day to ensure all the stages are balanced.

Much like Ahmed and Adel, a relationship manager can either have a healthy and balanced pipeline or a weak and out-of-control pipeline. Know that being an ultra-high performer throughout the year is entirely in your hands, and pipeline management is one of the main factors to focus on to achieve great results and unlock the next level of performance.

Chapter 19
PIPELINE VELOCITY

To have a resilient pipeline, one of the most important metrics to track is the pipeline velocity. It is defined as the speed at which the leads move through your pipeline, whether they close as won or lost. Pipeline velocity is an accurate and reliable tool to forecast your monthly revenue achievement.

PIPELINE VELOCITY CALCULATION

The following formula indicates the daily revenue projection: the number of opportunities in your pipeline (N_{op}) times the overall win-rate percentage ($WR_\%$) times the average deal size (DS_{avg}) divided by the current sales cycle (CSC):

$$Nop \times WR\% \times DSavg \div CSC$$

Multiply the answer from this equation by the number of working days, and you get the forecast for the month.

Let's look at an example. The total number of opportunities in the pipeline is 50, the overall win-rate percentage is 13 percent, the average deal size is $10,000 and the opportunities take 65 days to close. The pipeline velocity is at $1,000 daily. Multiply the figure by the number of working days, and you will get the monthly forecast of $1,000 × 25 = $25,000.

There are many metrics to work on to improve the pipeline velocity. Take a look at the table below:

Pipeline Velocity Table

.Metrics	Feb	March	April
Number of Opportunities	50	55	57
Win-Rate Percentage	13%	15%	15%
Average Deal Size	$10,000	$10,000	$12,000
Sale Cycle in Days	65	65	65
Daily Velocity	**$1,000.00**	**$1,269.23**	**$1,578.46**
Monthly Forecast × Working Days	$25,000.00	$31,730.77	$39,461.54

Looking at the number, the win rate improved from 13 percent to 15 percent in March, and the number of deals increased. As a result, the velocity figure moved up to $1,269 per day. In April, the win rate was maintained, but the average deal size was improved, and the number of deals increased, resulting in an enhancement in the average pipeline velocity to $1,578 daily.

USING PIPELINE VELOCITY IN FORECASTING

If you have been in sales for a long time, you know that forecasting is tricky. More often than not, many RMs miss their forecasts or their sales commitments by a greater margin. They provide projections based on gut feelings. Even worse, their commitment is dependent on one deal, and if that customer changes their mind, they are screwed.

The traditional way of forecasting is to take the average closed rate percentage and figure out the final closure. For example, if you have $20,000 in your hot bucket, you multiply this number by 80 percent and get the final figure, $16,000. This method seldom works because not all the opportunities in your hot stage will close in that particular month, if they get closed at all.

The more we use this methodology to forecast revenue, the less likely we are to hit our forecast. Forecasting should rely on the pipeline velocity calculation, as shown in the above table. Since the velocity is calculated daily, take the number and multiply it by the number of working days. If the daily number for April is $1,578 × 25 working days, your forecast for the month is $39,461. Once you eliminate the gut feeling and dependence on one deal, you will be able to forecast your monthly numbers accurately.

WAYS TO IMPROVE PIPELINE VELOCITY AND FORECASTING

You can enhance the pipeline velocity and conduct accurate forecasting if you manage the following metrics prudently:

Number of Qualified Opportunities in the Pipeline:

It's a simple fact to agree with: the number of opportunities in the pipeline shows you how healthy it is. The health of the pipeline or the number of opportunities therein directly impacts pipeline velocity, as it helps generate higher revenue.

You have control over prospecting. The more you prospect, the more opportunities you will create. On the other hand, premature deals don't deserve to be in the pipeline. The RM should ensure that only qualified deals enter the pipeline, and, yes, opportunities will get lost at some point in time. That is absolutely okay, but it doesn't mean that you lose 50 percent of the pipeline.

Win-Rate Percentage:

Enhancing the *win-rate percentage* will improve the pipeline velocity and forecast. Your win-rate percentage has a direct link to the number of qualified opportunities in the pipeline. Missing this one will create a significant gap in the pipeline.

We should develop a culture in which salespeople brag about the win-rate percentage. We should create healthy competition among the RMs and see who has a higher win-rate percentage quarterly and eventually annually.

Average Deal Size:

What is your go-to-market strategy? Who are you targeting, and what is their value? These are important questions to address before picking up the phone and prospecting. I assume you prefer to work with high-value customers to improve the average deal size. The last part of this book talks about how the product share of wallet enables you to connect with the right customer at the right time.

Sales Cycle in Days:

The faster we close the deal, the better our pipeline velocity will be. Think of a system to monitor the leads that hit your pipeline. Work on all the leads and strive to move the targeted ones to the active stage and then to the hot stage. This will happen only if you are proactive, take massive action, and never let the deals stall.

STALLED DEALS

We have all experienced the frustration of stalled deals. Many RMs throw good money after bad and keep chasing leads that have a low probability of closure. These deals have been stalled for more than five times the average sales cycle, and the RM is unsure how to go about it. Should she invest time and energy to revive these opportunities, or should she go hunt for new ones that will ultimately close?

The issue of stalled deals can have many causes. The most prominent one is being busy prospecting for new clients while forgetting that many opportunities already exist in the pipeline that are waiting to be moved to the next stage. Maybe, ironically, the RM thought the customer would call them back to move the deal forward for them.

I forgot how painful it was to think about stalled deals, and I usually go crazy when I see a big pipeline with no closure. Enough of this nonsense. It is time to fix this. Let us understand why opportunities get stalled in the first place, so you don't become a victim of it.

1- Invalid opportunities in the pipeline: RMs are under extreme pressure to generate leads and show a sizable pipeline. This is where they let unqualified deals creep into the pipeline to satisfy their line managers temporarily. They are unaware of the consequences of having a fake pipeline they know will not close.

2- The customer didn't understand the problems and the impact on their business: Remember, when there is no problem, there is no sale. Your deals might get stalled because you didn't articulate the impact of the problem in a way the client could easily grasp. Go back to the discovery stage and do it all over again.

3- No sense of urgency: If the first two points have been addressed, the deal is stalled because there is no sense of urgency. One of the best ways to create a sense of urgency is to stress the positive outcome of the proposed solution and the negative result if the status quo prevails. Case studies help demonstrate how other customers are avoiding the negative impacts and taking advantage of the benefits. Quantify the effect in a way that is easy to interpret and comprehend. On the other hand, the customer could have other priorities that are more important and urgent than addressing the existing issues. Perhaps the gap is not big enough to compel them to take immediate action.

4- The customer is talking to your competition: After identifying the problems and quantifying the impact, the customer is in lookout mode, trying to find multiple quotations from different vendors. Beware, this has to be managed carefully. Sometimes, the customer shows your proposal to other vendors to get a better price.

5- The customer lost interest: You have carefully managed all aspects of the deal, highlighted all the problems, and proposed the right solutions. You created a sense of urgency and managed the competition; however, the customer suddenly went dark for unknown reasons. There could be a chance that the customer is undergoing changes at multiple levels in the company. If this is the case, go back to the discovery stage of the sales process and do it all over again with the new contact.

Understanding why the deal is stalled is essential, so you can decide whether to pursue it or tag it as lost and shift your focus to opportunities that have a high probability of closure. Spend your time wisely on deals that will close. Realizing early that a deal is stalled is better than realizing it late.

VELOCITY CHART

How long does a deal stay in the first three stages of the pipeline (targeted, active, and hot) before it is considered stalled? What is the right pipeline velocity?

The table below shows controlled velocity versus uncontrolled pipeline velocity in the telecom industry selling digital products. The velocity shown here is based on an average sales cycle of thirty-five days. It all depends on what you sell; the velocity could vary at the product level. Align with your line manager and agree on a specific chart for your line of business.

Velocity Chart

Stage	7 Days	14 Days	30 Days
Targeted	In control	Attention	High attention
Active	In control	Attention	High attention
Hot	In control	Attention	High attention
Total number of days	21 days	42 days	90 days

On average, deals that stay in every stage for seven days are considered *controlled*. Deals that stay in every stage for fourteen days require immediate action because the overall number of days will reach forty-two from the lead generation date to closure. Deals that stay in each pipeline stage for thirty days require close attention because it would take up to ninety days to close a deal, which is considered high for certain products. Anything beyond these days is considered out of control.

The best-case scenario is a sales cycle of twenty-one days. A forty-two day scenario is considered acceptable, and you can still live with a ninety-day average closure sales cycle.

Not managing the pipeline velocity will lead to stalled deals. I know only one thing about stalled deals: sooner or later, these leads will land in the lost bucket.

Chapter 20
PIPELINE PRODUCT MIX

We have covered the pipeline size, balance, and velocity, but a healthy pipeline is not complete without addressing the *product mix*. The product mix is a true reflection of the RM's skillset and mindset. A healthy pipeline should include a good mix of products.

You will find yourself naturally gravitating toward a few products because you are comfortable selling them. It is not the wrong approach, but it indicates a skillset gap.

Depending on the industry, the number of opportunities per product matters. If you work for a company that sells many products, you should have a well-balanced product mix. Work with your line manager and decide which products you should focus on. For example, if you sell eight products, determine which products should get the primary focus and which should be secondary. Moreover, agree on the bare minimum number of opportunities across all products that should be registered in your pipeline.

Product Mix Table

Row	SMP	BAAS	Cloud	O365	SVT	VSaaS	Security	Total
RM1	5	3	10	0	3	3	30	54
RM2	2	0	3	20	12	2	0	39
RM3	3	1	3	1	0	0	0	8
RM4	0	0	0	29	6	10	35	80
RM5	13	3	3	20	2	1	0	42

The table shows some of the RMs don't have any opportunity or have a low number of deals in a specific product line. Here are some of the reasons RMs do not have a balanced product mix:

- They do not believe in the product.
- Their sales story is not as good as it should be.
- They lack product knowledge.
- They try one or two times and give up on the product.
- They are targeting the wrong customers.

Being stuck with two to three products because they are easy to sell and do not require much effort will impact your overall performance.

By focusing on only a few products, you will lose the opportunity to sell other products your clients need.

RESETTING YOUR PIPELINE

When the year finishes, congratulate yourself for a job well done. You are ready to get the closed and lost deals out of the pipeline and start the New Year carrying only the active opportunities—starting with a fresh and balanced pipeline.

Many relationship managers cling to stalled deals for a while and are afraid of getting them out of the pipeline. Sometimes, removing deals will affect the size of your pipeline. But let's be honest, having an average pipeline with qualified leads is better than having a fat, junky one.

Chapter 21

SALES PIPELINE MISTAKES TO AVOID

The performance gap widens between top producers and underperformers because of several mistakes that average salespeople make. It is necessary to know them upfront so you don't fall for them. Let's look at a few.

LETTING THE PIPELINE SHRINK—NO TIME FOR PROSPECTING

Relationship managers fail because they leave prospecting to whenever they have time. And guess what? They will never have time. Prospecting is a task that needs to be booked on your calendar daily and well in advance, and should be treated with the utmost priority.

Knowing when to prospect and how long to prospect is essential. The ideal situation is to prospect for two to three hours daily and never fall into the trap of, "I will prospect when I finish the tasks at hand." Make prospecting a priority. I know it is hard. It requires proactivity and courage to do it consistently. Look at it this way: If you stop prospecting, you will see your pipeline shrink. Not only that, but you also get into desperation mode and find yourself up against the universal law of need. Life doesn't like desperate people. The more desperate you are, the more difficult it will be to create opportunities and close deals.

UNQUALIFIED DEALS IN THE PIPELINE

I know you are under pressure to generate new leads, and your line manager is looking at the numbers on a weekly, if not daily basis, and you will be questioned if you don't meet the weekly lead generation numbers. I understand sometimes it is not possible to meet the lead generation target for one reason or another, but this doesn't mean that you put junk in the pipeline. Doing so will ruin the other pipeline metrics, from stalled deals and an imbalanced pipeline, to slow pipeline velocity and a high loss percentage.

How do I know that the deal is not qualified? Simply put, if your client doesn't agree that there is a problem to be addressed or an opportunity to be captured, it is not a qualified deal. If you are still not clear, reread the skillset part.

LOSING LEADS—NO FOCUS ON PIPELINE BALANCE

Average salespeople get so happy because they have a fat pipeline. But fat doesn't mean healthy, does it? Generating leads is one thing, but advancing the leads through the pipeline is another game plan altogether.

Ideally, spending two hours a day to advance the leads until they get closed is a good strategy. Another approach is to keep two to three days of focused activity on pipeline balance. Doing so will enable you to be on top of your pipeline.

AFRAID TO LOSE

After spending a ton of effort to generate leads, it is hard to push them out of the pipeline. Mediocre salespeople just cling to the deals that will not close and throw good money after bad. They've spent a lot of time on these deals, and they feel it is hard to let them go. If the deal is not going to close, there is nothing much you can do. This is what sales is all about. You win many deals, but at the same time, you lose a few of them.

The lost stage should not exceed 25 percent of your pipeline by the end of the year. If it does, it indicates that you are not qualifying the leads properly to begin with. Remember, not every opportunity deserves to be in your pipeline.

CRACKING THE SALES CODE

THE SECRET FORMULA TO UNLOCK YOUR SALES POTENTIAL IN BUSINESS SALES

Part IV
TOOLSET

Chapter 22

PRODUCT SHARE OF WALLET

Now that we have covered so much ground, the sales mindset, skillset, sales story, and pipeline management, it is time to roll back to an essential weapon in our arsenal: *the product share of wallet.*

The product share of wallet is a document that encompasses all the information you have gathered in a specific format during your phone calls or meetings with customers. It is a blueprint for your go-to-market strategy in the future. It enables you to be in front of the right customer at the right time, selling them the right product, most of the time. The product share of wallet provides a 360-degree view across all products for every customer you manage. It is a must-have tool. Without it, the formula for being successful in sales will not be complete.

SNIPER RIFLE OR MACHINE GUN?

Do you have a sniper rifle or a machine gun?

In a sniper rifle approach, it takes only one bullet to bring the target down. A sniper's first shot hit the target 95 percent of the time. Snipers stay focused and shoot when the right time comes. On the other hand, a machine gun approach is all about targeting anyone who comes your way, not necessarily following any strategy—but shooting without any focus and praying that you eventually hit someone. The issue with this approach is twofold. First, it's a waste of resources in terms of time and effort. Second, there is frustration in targeting everyone but not getting the desired results.

Knowing your targeted list of customers takes away the stress and pressure that comes with sales. The product share of wallet is a place where you start to formulate multiple plans of attack. It is your blueprint to market that guides you to the easiest targets to hit first and enables you to be in front of the right customer at the right time, selling the right product.

Imagine if you have this level of clarity: Looking at your product share of wallet, you should be able to highlight the right customers to target with a particular product in a specific month. For example, here are potential opportunities for September: four cloud solutions, three security solutions, and four online marketing solutions. Honestly, I don't know of any other tool that could make you more efficient and productive in your go-to-market strategy than the product share of wallet.

Average salespeople have no plan. They are not effective nor productive because they either meet the wrong customers or sell the wrong products. They get their product share of wallet filled just because someone else tells them to do so. They don't understand the importance of this document until eight months down the road when the information about the customers is captured in a manner that can be leveraged upon. There is another group of underperformers who completely miss the idea. They simply input wrong information in the product share of wallet, just to finish the activity and hand it over to their line managers. The same group of underperformers struggle and keep going back to the wrong customers time and time again, and then complain that nothing is working and start to blame everyone and everything around them but themselves.

BUILDING THE PRODUCT SHARE OF WALLET

How you build your product share of wallet depends on the company you work for. Some companies utilize big data analytics to generate targeted lists of customers to enable the sales team to formulate an accurate attack for every product they sell, while in other companies, the sales team builds their own. However, complementing the big data analytics by gathering relevant information from the customer to plan an attack is an effective strategy.

Building a comprehensive product share of wallet requires time. If you manage fifty accounts and have ten products to sell, it will probably take between five and seven months to complete the product share of wallet. It requires discipline to get it done, simply because you do not get an immediate return on investment for your time. Hang in there, stay focused, and see how your productivity score skyrockets after getting the product share of wallet completed.

The first step in building the product share of wallet is prospecting, which means you have to go through the traditional sales process. You don't want to seem like a contact center agent by only calling and filling in the details. Go through the typical sales cycle first, and then get the details in a well-thought-out format.

Let us assume you intend to call a client to go through the cloud sales story. You won't be surprised if the customer says no to your proposition, will you? Of course not. We have discussed the first objection the customer will always throw at you, and we all agree that it's normal. Now, following the objection, the first thing to learn is *why* the customer said no. Write down the details for future reference so you can come back prepared to address the objections. Second, take the customer through a set of questions that you want the answers to, if not discovered during the discovery process.

Pre-Pipeline Stage:

Once your product share of wallet is complete, it will be your pre-pipeline stage. The table below shows a sample of information gathered for five customers for a VSaaS (video surveillance as a service) product. Let's examine which customer is worth targeting and which customer should be put on hold for now.

VSaaS Share of Wallet

Customer	# Cameras	One-time charge	Annual maintenance	Storage	How old is the camera?	Remarks
Customer A	10	$25,000	$3,000	Cloud	12 months	Customer is not willing to move because he has just invested $25K. July 3, 2021
Customer B	20	$10,000	0	Local	7 years	10 cameras are faulty, customer shown some interest. August 12, 2021
Customer C	0					No cameras. September 20, 2021. Customer has potential for 40 cameras.
Customer D	30	$30,000	$6,000	Local	5 years	Customer is looking to upgrade his cameras and wants advanced analytics. He is also complaining about the quality of the cameras. Their contract with the vendor will expire in December 2022.
Customer E	3	$500	0	Local	3	Small setup.

Looking at the above VSaaS share of wallet, which customer is the right one to target? I would say customers B, C, and D. Let's look at every customer in turn.

Customer A: They may not be an immediate target, as they invested $25K a year ago. Unless they have a problem with their cameras or vendor, they won't be interested in a change. The customer can be looked at next year, but they are not the right one to target now.

Customer B: They have the potential to buy since the cameras are quite old, out of which ten cameras are faulty. The customer is also not satisfied with their current vendor. This customer could be an immediate target.

Customer C: Green-field customer; they do not have cameras. We could take the customer through the sales story and try to identify the gaps. This customer could be part of the targeted list of customers. But before we do that, we need to understand how many cameras they require; if the requirement is small, we should probably focus our time and attention somewhere else.

Customer D: They have the potential to buy. They are looking to upgrade their cameras and would like to have advanced analytics. However, they are still under contract, which will end after fourteen months. We can approach the customer four months prior to the expiry date of the agreement.

Customer E: The customer has a small setup. Maybe this lead is not worth pursuing.

Top performers will spend their time with customers B and C while returning to customer D closer to the contract expiry date. They will re-evaluate customer A in the subsequent year and will not target customer E since the opportunity is small.

PRODUCT SHARE OF WALLET ADOPTION—AHMED VS. ADEL

Going back to the pipeline balance, you will notice that Adel had a healthier and more well-balanced pipeline compared to Ahmed. The difference in pipeline health is primarily due to the different approaches both took. Let's evaluate how Ahmed and Adel have created and used the product share of wallet.

To clarify, Ahmed and Adel joined the team on the same day, and their line manager explained to them the benefits of having a comprehensive product share of wallet. They were also shown how to get it done and how best they could utilize it.

Ahmed's Approach

Ahmed started to fill in the details after every sales call. After doing so for two months, he lost interest and saw no value in the activity. Therefore, he dropped it.

Things spiraled out of control and Ahmed got desperate to generate leads and started to approach customers randomly again, and as a result, he ended up meeting the wrong customers, who were not immediate targets. Ahmed was under extreme pressure to show progress on building his pipeline and close. He kept going back to the wrong customers time and time again with no idea who to target. He had no clue what to do or who to talk to. After nine months, his line manager put him on a PIP (performance improvement plan), and in less than a year, he was fired!

Adel's Approach

On the other hand, Adel had been working very hard on building a robust product share of wallet. He filled in the details and captured every little bit of information about his clients religiously. Adel was not getting an immediate return on investment on his time but benefited from the little information he had captured all along.

Adel created a targeted list of customers for every product from the little information he had gathered. As a result, he built a healthy pipeline and managed to achieve his target. After nine months of hard work in building a resilient product share of wallet, Adel now has a 360-degree view of his accounts and can easily identify the right customers to target. The product share of wallet has enabled him to become one of the top performers in the team and helped him over-achieve his target consistently over the past 4 quarters.

Here is how Adel is benefiting from his product share of wallet:

- Adel creates a targeted list of customers for every product every month and works according to the plan.

- He knows who not to target at all, especially the ones with low revenue.

- He only reapproaches the customers who have a high probability of conversion.

- He knows precisely how much the customer is paying the competitor and can develop a strategy to win the customer's account.

- He knows the expiry date of the clients' contract, if any, so he targets them just at the right time.

Having such clarity about the business setup of his clients gives Adel a competitive edge, enabling him to become efficient and productive in his go-to-market strategy. Here is a question: Whose approach would you like to follow, Ahmed's or Adel's?

WHAT OTHER TOOLS SHOULD BE IN YOUR TOOLKIT?

The product share of wallet is one example of many tools you could have in your sales toolkit. Depending on the industry you operate in and the company you work for, your requirements would be unique and different from other salespeople's.

The description of every tool is not covered in this book. I want you to think about all the tools that would enable you to be a successful sales professional and try to incorporate them into your daily routine. Here are a few examples to start with:

1- CRM (customer relationship management): information about the clients and opportunity management portal

2- Sales intelligence: details on contracts, amount spent, purchase history, etc.

3- Sales analytics: built on top of the CRM to provide leads, trends, and sales forecasts

4- Sales enablement: a portal that includes training, product information, case studies, lessons learned, customer testimonials, big-win references, and readymade proposals

5- CPQ (configure, price, and quote) software

The above tools must be provided by the company you work for, and some of these tools are costly and may not be provided to you in the short term. The availability of these tools would definitely help achieve a higher level of efficiency and productivity, but their absence should not be a show-stopper. The good news is that the product share of wallet we talked about doesn't need a budget to build. All you need to get started in sales is a spreadsheet of your product share of wallet, a mobile phone, a laptop, and a video calling platform—and don't forget your mindset and skillset. That's it.

Chapter 23
SALES BUSINESS PLAN

Congratulations if you have come this far—it indicates you are either one of the top performers or at least have a strong desire to be among the top players.

Now that you know what it takes to be an ultra-high performer in sales, it is time to put what we have learned into one document that will govern your roadmap to success.

One of the best ways to ensure that we plan and execute successfully is to write down the *sales business plan*. We have all read studies that suggest people who write their goals are more successful than people who don't. The sales business plan shows you the bigger picture of how to approach success over a period of one year.

The sales business plan comes in many shapes and forms, but there are five key elements I ask salespeople to include in their plan. They are the basic elements of the sales success formula: goal, mindset, skillset, pipeline, and the product share of wallet.

WHAT?

Goals:

What do you aspire to achieve? The plan should declare your personal goals for the year.

What is your annual target? Break it down quarterly and monthly or, if possible, weekly. For example, $100,000 is the annual target, $8,000 is the monthly target, and $2,000 is the weekly closure target.

HOW?

We discussed earlier that the higher-level goals can't be managed directly but can be influenced by mid-level goals and driven by low-level goals. Your low-level and mid-level goals should be in alignment with the high-level goals. If you plan to achieve $100K annually, the daily activities must be designed to take you to the top-level goals. Write down the list of activities with which your goals will be attainable if planned and managed the correct way.

MINDSET EVALUATION:

On a scale of 1 to 5, how do you evaluate yourself from a mindset perspective? Sometimes, the evaluation will be subjective, so check if you can back your evaluation up with real examples.

Mindset Evaluation Example:

Scale	1 to 5	Goal
Discipline	4	5
Proactivity	3	5
Positivity	2.5	5
Persistence	3	5
Relationship	4	5
Growth	2	5

What is your action plan to improve the score of every element mentioned above, and by when? Write them down and then decide on the next mindset evaluation date. Ideally, the self-evaluation activity should be carried out on a weekly basis to track your progress and improve.

SKILLSET DEVELOPMENT

We discussed the importance of skillset development in the previous chapters; it is time to write down the plan.

Here are a few questions to consider. They are not comprehensive in any way:

1- On what products do I need to improve my knowledge?

2- On what products do I have to improve my sales story?

3- In what courses will I register myself?

4- How many books will I read in the next year?

5- What types of books will I read?

6- How many audiobooks will I listen to in the next year?

7- In which domain will I get myself certified?

8- Which subject should I know more about to enhance my business acumen?

Here is an example of a product development plan. Do the same for the rest of the questions.

Monthly Plan

Month 1	Month 2	Month 3
O365	M2M	Cloud
Online marketing	SVT	Data center

PIPELINE MANAGEMENT ACTIVITIES

Prospecting Target

Ask yourself: How much new business do I plan to generate over one year? Then break it down into monthly, weekly, and daily targets. For example, if you plan to generate $240K annually, break it down monthly, which is $20K, and then daily, which comes to $1,000 worth of business every day if we assume you have twenty-one working days.

Knowing your plan is one thing, and how you would achieve it is a totally different thing. What does it take to prospect $1,000 worth of business every day?

- How many phone calls should you make per day?

- How many virtual meetings should you conduct per day?
- How many physical meetings should you conduct per day?

Pipeline Balance

We discussed the importance of maintaining a perfect pipeline balance to avoid desperation by the end of the month and to avoid performance rollercoasters by the end of the quarter.

The pipeline balance plan must be laid down well in advance. Here is an example of what goes into your sales business plan. Keep an eye on your pipeline balance daily and strive to set it at 30 percent at targeted stage, 30 percent at active stage, 20 percent at hot stage, and 20 percent at closed stage in the first quarter of the year. The second quarter may be different in terms of percentages, and so will quarters three and four.

Answer the following questions:

- How many deals will you move from targeted to active stage every day?
- How many deals will you move from active to hot stage every day?
- How many deals will you move from hot to closed stage every day?

Product Balance/Mix

What products should go into your pipeline? Focusing on all products may not be possible. However, achieving the right balance is key. If your company product portfolio consists of ten different products, decide which product will be your primary focus and which ones will be secondary in alignment with your line manager.

Here is an example:

Primary Focus

- Smart messaging
- Online marketing
- VSaaS
- SVT
- Cloud

Secondary Focus

- Data center
- M2M

The two most important questions to answer about the product mix are as follows:

- How many opportunities should I create in every product category?
- How many opportunities should I close in every product category?

Think about the answer and work toward achieving the right mix and balance across the entire product portfolio.

Pipeline Velocity

It is essential to monitor the pipeline velocity to avoid stagnated deals. The more you wait, the more deals will land in the lost bucket. Deciding on a strategy to manage pipeline velocity is crucial. Here are a few questions you need to consider:

1- What is the threshold for the targeted stage? How many days can the leads stay there, and at what level are they considered stalled?

2- What is the threshold for the active stage? How many days can the leads stay there, and at what level are they considered stalled?

3- What is the threshold for the hot stage? How many days can the leads stay in this stage, and at what level are they considered stalled?

Here are a few more questions to ask yourself in order to manage the velocity of the pipeline:

- How often will you check the stagnated deals?
- What will you do to ensure leads don't cross their threshold level?
- What action will you take if the leads cross their threshold level?

THE PRODUCT SHARE OF WALLET

Creating a targeted list of customers is just one filter away. You get to choose who to target and when to target them. Getting the product share of wallet completed will require a plan of action on your part. Here are a few questions to ask first:

- What product should I profile first?
- How many customers should I profile every day?
- What kind of information should I gather?
- How will the information help me target the right customers at the right time?
- How long should I spend on this activity on a daily, weekly, and monthly basis?

You can elaborate more on the completion plan of the product share of wallet. Once you are done with this activity, enjoy being more effective in your go-to-market strategy, become an ultra-high performer in your domain, and crush any quote that comes your way.

CONCLUSION

I have a confession to make. Sales is the hardest yet the easiest job in the world. Selling *should* be easy, but when salespeople don't follow through with proper execution, they make the job harder than it needs to be. Now you have the code that unlocks the secrets that are never shared by the top performers. Follow through and watch yourself rise above all. The MST framework discussed in this book is straightforward. Nevertheless, its implementation takes time. It takes a massive amount of time and effort to nurture a healthy mindset, build a robust skillset, and develop an effective toolset.

Being in the trenches and working alongside sixty sales professionals gave rise to many of the practical ideas I have shared in this book. These ideas can catalyze your success in the market.

It must have been an exciting journey as you flipped through the pages. But let's sum it up for you. The first part of the book discussed the fundamentals of sales. It shed light on the MST framework, the sales process, and the reason why most salespeople struggle.

We agreed that the primary role of the RM is to highlight the problems and issues the customer faces. Discussing anything other than what is important to the customer does not help much. The customer is interested in knowing what's in it for them before learning about your product or solution. If you think these are the basics of sales, you are right. However, this doesn't always come as common sense for a lot of salespeople out there. Mediocre sales reps start the discussion with their product first and never talk about the customer's issues or opportunities.

The second part of the book talked about the first pillar of the MST framework, which is mindset. Mindset is everything; it either makes or breaks the salesperson. Being aware of your state of mind is critical because your path to success starts with mindset. Managing one's mindset ensures everything else falls in place. Below are the building blocks of a sales-driven mindset.

It all starts with *discipline*. This is the mother of all traits. Without discipline, it is hard to propel oneself forward. Lack of discipline leads to procrastination. You will see yourself with a new habit, and before you know it, you will fall back to your old way of doing things. Salespeople should learn and understand the importance of delayed gratification because nothing in sales happens overnight. Reaching your goals takes time, building relationships takes time, sharpening your skillset takes time, creating a pipeline takes time, everything in sales takes time.

Proactive sales professionals take charge of their careers. They don't wait for things to happen to them; they make things happen. Top achievers take control of their calendar, protect it from non-sales-related activities, and ensure that their time is devoted to one thing—selling. Reactive salespeople seldom succeed in sales. Nothing happens when you wait—but when you act.

Ultra-high performers know the importance of being positive simply because *positivity* opens up new possibilities in their careers. They understand that sales comes with challenges. Nonetheless, they stay positive and see the light on the horizon. On the other hand, pessimistic salespeople ride performance rollercoasters and allow negativity to control their lives. They are far from attaining their annual goals and put the blame on everything except themselves.

Sales professionals understand that nothing gets closed from the first round of discussion. Being *persistent* is the key that unlocks opportunities that seem difficult to crack in the first place. Don't settle for mediocrity, and do not take no for an answer.

People do business with people they know and like. Building meaningful *relationships* with your customers and leveling up to the C-suite executives unlocks opportunities you never imagined possible. It is hard, but once you get there, you will enjoy a successful sales career. As the saying goes, "Out of sight, out of mind."

The last thing about the mindset is to *learn and grow*. If you are not growing, you are dying. Let me break it to you: If you are not investing in yourself by learning everything about sales, it's better to quit. Maybe you could succeed elsewhere, but definitely not in sales.

The third part of the book talked about building a sales skillset. It is essential to get equipped with the right weapon to go to market well prepared. You don't want to fight with a knife when your opponent has a gun. Many customers know more about the technologies, products, and services than the salesperson. Don't let a lack of business acumen get in the way. Your sales story is your primary weapon and ally in the market. Sharpen it until it comes naturally to you. Once the opportunity finds its way to your pipeline, deploy your pipeline management skills as explained in this book. Manage them well, and closure is nothing but an inevitable outcome.

The last part of the book was about possessing the right toolset. The product share of wallet is an essential tool that enables you to be in front of the right customer at the right time, selling the right product. It increases the relationship manager's productivity exponentially. Building it takes time, but once it's complete, you will enjoy a new world of opportunities at your fingertips.

Now you know the rules of the sales game and the formula ultra-high performers use. The secret is out, and I firmly believe there is no reason for anyone to fail in sales. By now, you know that there is no magic pill that will turn you into an IRONMAN. You have to put in the work to be successful. The results will not be visible for the first few months. Hang in there—it will ultimately pay off.

Sales is fun. Enjoy your work. My final advice is to dream BIG and make efforts. Change history and write your own success story. Good luck, and I wish you all the best.

I would like to hear from you. Connect with me on:

crackingsalescode@gmail.com

00971507177714

APPENDIX

APPENDIX ONE:

SHARE OF WALLET FORMAT

Below is an example of a share of wallet format for vehicle tracking solution. You can come up with your own format for every product you are planning to have a game plan for.

COMPNAY NAME	INDUSTRY TYPE	NUMBER OF CARS	SOLUTION USED	VENDOR NAME	CURRENT SPEND	CONTRACT EXPIRY DATE	REMARKS
ABC	Retail	30	No solution used				Approach
XYZ	Contracting	50	Third party solution	RBA	$30,000	01-Mar-23	Attack prior to expiry date
CCB	Hospitality	1	No solution used				Low value deal

APPENDIX TWO:

SALES STORY EXAMPLES

Cloud Sales Story

PART-1: Find the Gap

Setting Expectation:

Hi Ameer, I would like to talk about a solution that I believe will add value to your company. In order to explore that with you, I will be asking a few questions to check if our solution is a perfect fit for your company. To understand and evaluate the situation, I will need about twenty-five minutes to discuss the challenges and goals. Will that work for you?

Probing:

- Where are your servers hosted?
- Do you have any disaster recovery in place?

Agreement and Power Statement:

I agree with you, many companies in your industry host their servers in-house. I would like to share with you that IT managers in your industry say that there are a few challenges associated with hosting the servers in-house.

- Business continuity concerns (power disconnection, Internet disconnection, fire breakout, and hardware failure)
- Security concerns and malware attacks
- Resource constraint and high cost
- Ineffective resource allocation
- Third-party risks

Ask:

A: Have you experienced any of these challenges before?

B: What is the plan if any of these risks happen?

Discovery:

I would like to do a little activity to show you the issues other customers in your industry are facing and the impact of these risks on their business. We will then evaluate together if these risks and issues are relevant to your business or not.

Discovery #1: Current State of the Customer (You can share the issues with the customer, but ask them to identify the impact.)

Issues, Concerns, Risks	Impact of Issues	Root Cause
• Business continuity issues • Security issues • Over dependency on third party • Ineffective resource allocation • High cost	• Business interruption • Loss of data • Loss of money • Being hostage to a third part	• On-premises hosting

Ask Provocative Questions:

Ask provocative questions throughout the discovery stage, such as:

- Do you think these risks are relevant to your business?
- What will be the impact of fire or any other risks on your business?

- Could you walk me through the steps you take to prevent loss of data in case of hardware failure?
- How often do you buy new hardware?

Discovery #2: Future State of the Customer

Great, I would like to share with you the experience of other customers after moving their servers to the cloud.

*Note: Work with the customer to quantify the impact.

Opportunities	Positive Impact	Quantify Positive Impact
• Little or no management is required • Risk-free environment • Business continuity assurance • No maintenance is required • Easy to scale up or down	• Peace of mind • Focus on important tasks • No risk of downtime • Fast deployment • Cost savings on management • Cost savings on maintenance	• Refer to cost/benefit analysis below

Build Urgency

Share a case study:

One of the real estate companies that I manage has been in business for the past fifteen years and just recently got hacked, and the hacker asked for $300,000 to give them their data back. I am sure nobody wants to be in this situation.

Engaging the Right Stakeholders:

Is there anybody in your company we should involve to explain the risks and the opportunities?

COST/BENEFIT ANALYSIS

Doing this activity with the customer will take twenty to thirty minutes. It's important to prepare the customer's mind before jumping into the discussion. The customer should understand what you are up to because you will be asking many questions.

Cost/Benefit Analysis Example:

Current Setup	Current Cost	Proposed Solution	Proposed Cost – 30 Users
Active directory	$2,000	Active directory on SaaS	30×25 = $750
Firewall		Security solution	30×25 = $750
Exchange server		O365	30×20 = $600
Accounting server		SAGE	$1,000 (10 licenses)
Share point server		Inclusive with O365	
Database server		Goes to virtual machine	$2,000
Application server		Goes to virtual machine	$2,000
Third-party charges	$3,000	Third party will manage only the virtual machines – thus, their scoop will be reduced by 50%	$1,500
Utility bill	$3,000	Since all servers will move out of the office, there is no utility bill for the servers	0
Human resource cost – two people	$10,000	Only one is needed; the other one can be utilized somewhere else in the company	$5,000
Risk-free environment – opportunity cost	$3,000	Customer will be in a risk-free environment	0
Amortization cost over five years	$700	No need to invest in hardware in the future	0
Total	**$21,700**		**$12,700**

The above is just an example. Numbers will change depending on the situation.

Important—Summarize the Problem Before You Go to the Second Part:

Note: You should not go to the second part if you can't articulate the issues and the challenges and the customer should agree that these risks may occur.

PART 2: Bridge the Gap

Show the customer how you can help bridge the gaps.

Solution

Great, I would like to share with you the experience of other customers after considering the solution:

- Five layers of redundancy on power
- Two layers of redundancy on Internet
- Multiple layers of cloud security
- High availability on cloud machines

Demo

- Showcase a demo or share references

Differentiation

- Cloud environment is hosted in the country
- Monthly recurring charges
- 24/7 support by CCIE engineers
- High availability of cloud environment
- Fixed cost
- Easy to upgrade or downgrade
- Etc....

Pricing

You are now ready to share the offer.

APPENDIX THREE:

COACHING FORM

Coaching Session

Name:

Coaching date:

Performance Review

Monthly Performance- overall

	Jan	Feb	Mar	Apr	May	Jun	Jul	Total
Target								
Ach.								
%								

Performance (Product wise)

	Jan	Feb	Mar	Apr	May	Jun	Jul	Total
Target								
Ach.								
%								

Pipeline Balance View

	Qualify	Proposal	Hot	Submitted	closed	Lost	Total
Value							
% of total							

Product Mix

	SMP	BaaS	Cloud	M2M	O365	Total
Count						
Value						

CALENDAR SNAPSHOT

What does the calendar look like for the next 7 days?

Activity Week Wise

	Week One	Week Two	Week Three
Physical Visit			
Virtual Visit			
Calls			

Commitment: What is coming next week?

	Week One	Week Two	Week Three
Product One			
Product Two			
Product Three			

Self-Development Plan

	Week One	Week Two	Week Three
Product			
Role Plays			

FOCUS ACTIVITIES FOR THIS WEEK

CLEAR NEXT STEP

REFERENCES

Cialdini, Robert. 2006. *Influence: The Psychology of Persuasion*. New York: Harper Business.

Covey, R. Steven. 2017. *The 7 Habits of Highly Effective People: Powerful lessons in Personal Change*. Simon & Schuster.

Duhigg, Charles. 2014. *The power of Habit: Why We Do What We Do in Life and Business*. New York: Random House.

Goleman, Daniel. 2005. *Emotional Intelligence: Why it Can Matter More Than IQ*. New York: Bantam.

Carnegie, Dale. 2006. *How to Win Friends and Influence People*. Vermilion.

KEENAN. *2018. Gap Selling: Getting the Customer to Yes*. Sales guy.com.

Salz, B. Lee. 2021. *Sell Different: Sales Differentiation Strategies to Outsmart, Outmaneuver, & Outsell the Competition*. HarperCollins Leadership.

Iannarino, Anthony. 2017. *The Lost Art of Closing: Winning the Ten Commitments that drive sales*. Portfolio.

Duckworth, Angela. 2017. *Grit: Why Passion and Resilience are the Secrets to Success*. Ebury Publishing.

Dweck, S, Carol. 2017. *Mindset: Changing the Way You Think to Fulfil Your Potential*. Robinson.

Sink, Simon. 2011. *Start with why: How Great Leaders Inspire Everyone to Take Action*. Imusti.

References

Cardone, Grant. 2012. *Sell or be sold: How to Get Your Way in Business and Life*. Greenleaf Book Group.

Belfort, Jordan. 2018. *Way of the wolf: Straight Line Selling*. Gallery Books.

Blount, Jeb. 2017. *Sale EQ: How ultra-High Performers Leverage Sales Specific Emotional Intelligence to Close the Complex deal*. John Wiley & Sons Inc.

Clear, James. 2018. *Atomic Habits: An Easy & Proven Way to Build Good Habits & Break Bad Ones*. Avery Publishing Group.

Rosen, Keith. 2018. *Sales Leadership: The Essential Leadership Framework to Coach Sales Champions, Inspire Excellence, and Exceed Your Business Goals*. John Wiley & Sons Inc.

Stanley, Colleen. *2020. Emotional Intelligence for Sales Leadership: The Secret to Building High-Performance Sales Teams*. HarperCollins Leadership.

Jordan, Jason. & Vazzana, Michelle. *2011. Cracking the Sales Management Code: The Secrets to Measuring and Managing Sales Performance*. McGraw-Hill Professional.

Weinberg, Mike. *2018. New Sales Simplified: The Essential Handbook For Prospecting and New Business Development*. Amacom.

Stanley, Colleen. 2018. *Emotional Intelligence for Sales Success: Connect with Customers and Get Results*. Amacom.

Iannarino, Anthony. 2016. *The Only Sales guide you'll ever need*: Portfolio.

Hunter, Mark. 2020. *A Mind for Sales: Daily Habits and Practical Strategies for Sales Success*. HarperCollins Leadership.

Pink, H. Daniel. 2013. *To Sell is Human: The Surprising Truth About Moving Others*. Riverhead Books.

Dixon, Mathew. & Adamson, Brent. *2011. The Challenger Sales: Taking Control Of The Customer Conversation*. Portfolio.

Brown, Berne. 2012. *Power of Vulnerability: Teachings on Authenticity, Connection and Courage*. Sound Tru Inc.

Cuddy, Amy. 2018. *Presence: Bringing Your Boldest Self to Your Biggest Challenge*. Little, Brown Spark.

Fenton, Richard. & Waltz, Andrea. 2007. *Go for No: Yes Is The Destination No Is How You Get There*. Accelerated Performance Training.

Bradberry, Travis. & Greaves, Jean. 2009. E*motional Intelligence 2.0: Harness The Power of The #1 Predictor Of Success.* Enhanced.

Tracy, Brian. 2016. *The Psychology of Selling: Increase Your Sales Faster and Easier Than You Ever Thought Possible.* HarperCollins Leadership.

Abraham, Keith.2019. *It Starts With Passion: Do What You Love And Love What You Do.* John Wiley & Sons Australia.

Rackham, Neil. 2000. *Spin Selling: The Best-Validated Sales Method Available Today. Developed From Research Studies Of 35,000 Sales Calls. Used By The Top Salesforce across the world.* High bridge Audio and Blackstone Publishing.

Weinberg, Mike. 2020. *Sales Truth: Debunk the Myths. Apply Powerful Principles. Win More New Sales.* HarperCollins & Leadership.